JAMESTOWN EDUCATION

MW00999461

TIMED READINGS

Third Edition

Fifty 400-Word Passages
with Questions for
Building Reading Speed

BOOK TWO

Edward Spargo

Mc Graw Hill **Glencoe McGraw-Hill**

New York, New York   Columbus, Ohio   Chicago, Illinois   Peoria, Illinois   Woodland Hills, California

JAMESTOWN EDUCATION

Titles in This Series
Timed Readings, Third Edition
Timed Readings in Literature
Timed Readings Plus

Glencoe/McGraw-Hill
A Division of The McGraw·Hill Companies

Timed Readings, Third Edition
Book Two

Cover and text design: Deborah Hulsey Christie

ISBN: 0-89061-504-7

Send all queries:
Glencoe/McGraw-Hill
8787 Orion Place
Columbus, OH 43240-4027

Manufactured in the United States of America

17 18 19 20 21 22 ROV 11 10

Contents

Introduction to the Student

These *Timed Readings* are designed to help you become a faster and better reader. As you progress through the book, you will find yourself growing in reading speed and comprehension. You will be challenged to increase your reading rate while maintaining a high level of comprehension.

Reading, like most things, improves with practice. If you practice improving your reading speed, you will improve. As you will see, the rewards of improved reading speed will be well worth your time and effort.

Why Read Faster?

The quick and simple answer is that faster readers are better readers. Does this statement surprise you? You might think that fast readers would miss something and their comprehension might suffer. This is not true, for two reasons:

1. Faster readers comprehend faster. When you read faster, the writer's message is coming to you faster and makes sense sooner. Ideas are interconnected. The writer's thoughts are all tied together, each one leading to the next. The more quickly you can see how ideas are related to each other, the more quickly you can comprehend the meaning of what you are reading.

2. Faster readers concentrate better. Concentration is essential for comprehension. If your mind is wandering you can't understand what you are reading. A lack of concentration causes you to re-read, sometimes over and over, in order to comprehend. Faster readers concentrate better because there's less time for distractions to interfere. Comprehension, in turn, contributes to concentration. If you are concentrating and comprehending, you will not become distracted.

Want to Read More?

Do you wish that you could read more? (or, at least, would you like to do your required reading in less time?) Faster reading will help.

The illustration on the next page shows the number of books someone might read over a period of ten years. Let's see what faster reading could do for you. Look at the stack of books read by a slow reader and the stack

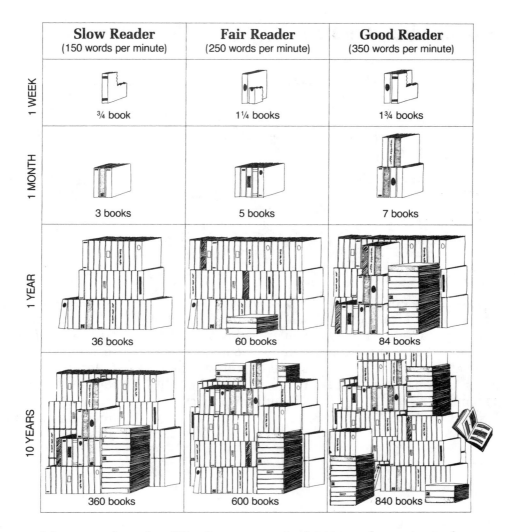

	Slow Reader (150 words per minute)	Fair Reader (250 words per minute)	Good Reader (350 words per minute)
1 WEEK	¾ book	1¼ books	1¾ books
1 MONTH	3 books	5 books	7 books
1 YEAR	36 books	60 books	84 books
10 YEARS	360 books	600 books	840 books

read by a good reader. (We show a speed of 350 words a minute for our "good" reader, but many fast readers can more than double that speed.) Let's say, however, that you are now reading at a rate of 150 words a minute. The illustration shows you reading 36 books a year. By increasing your reading speed to 250 words a minute, you could increase the number of books to 60 a year.

We have arrived at these numbers by assuming that the readers in our illustration read for one hour a day, six days a week, and that an average book is about 72,000 words long. Many people do not read that much, but they might if they could learn to read better and faster.

Faster reading doesn't *take* time, it *saves* time!

How to Use This Book

1 Learn the Four Steps
Study and learn the four steps to follow to become a better and faster reader. The steps are covered on pages 9, 10, 11, and 12.

2 Preview
Turn to the selection you are going to read and wait for the instructor's signal to preview. Your instructor will allow 30 seconds for previewing.

3 Begin reading
When your instructor gives you the signal, begin reading. Read at a slightly faster-than-normal speed. Read well enough so that you will be able to answer questions about what you have read.

7 Fill in the progress graph
Enter your score and plot your reading time on the graph on page 118 or 119. The right-hand side of the graph shows your words-per-minute reading speed. Write this number at the bottom of the page on the line labeled *Words per Minute*.

4 Record your time

When you finish reading, look at the blackboard and note your reading time. Your reading time will be the lowest time remaining on the board, or the next number to be erased. Write this time at the bottom of the page on the line labeled *Reading Time*.

5 Answer the questions

Answer the ten questions on the next page. There are five fact questions and five thought questions. Pick the *best* answer to each question and put an x in the box beside it.

6 Correct your answers

Using the Answer Key on pages 116 and 117, correct your work. Circle your wrong answers and put an x in the box you should have marked. Score 10 points for each correct answer. Write your score at the bottom of the page on the line labeled *Comprehension Score*.

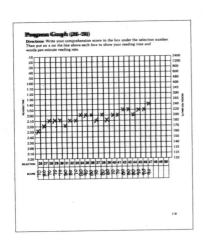

Instructions for the Pacing Drills

From time to time your instructor may wish to conduct pacing drills using *Timed Readings*. For this work you need to use the Pacing Dots printed in the margins of your book pages. The dots will help you regulate your reading speed to match the pace set by your instructor or announced on the reading cassette tape.

You will be reading at the correct pace if you are at the dot when your instructor says "Mark" or when you hear a tone on the tape. If you are ahead of the pace, read a little more slowly; if you are behind the pace, increase your reading speed. Try to match the pace exactly.

Follow these steps.

Step 1: Record the pace. At the bottom of the page, write on the line labeled *Words per Minute* the rate announced by the instructor or by the speaker on the tape.

Step 2: Begin reading. Wait for the signal to begin reading. Read at a slightly faster-than-normal speed. You will not know how on-target your pace is until you hear your instructor say "Mark" or until you hear the first tone on the tape. After a little practice you will be able to select an appropriate starting speed most of the time.

Step 3: Adjust your pace. As you read, try to match the pace set by the instructor or the tape. Read more slowly or more quickly as necessary. You should be reading the line beside the dot when you hear the pacing signal. The pacing sounds may distract you at first. Don't worry about it. Keep reading and your concentration will return.

Step 4: Stop and answer questions. Stop reading when you are told to, even if you have not finished the selection. Answer the questions right away. Correct your work and record your score on the line *Comprehension Score*. Strive to maintain 80 percent comprehension on each drill as you gradually increase your pace.

Step 5: Fill in the pacing graph. Transfer your words-per-minute rate to the box labeled *Pace* on the pacing graph on page 120. Then plot your comprehension score on the line above the box.

These pacing drills are designed to help you become a more flexible reader. They encourage you to "break out" of a pattern of reading everything at the same speed.

The drills help in other ways, too. Sometimes in a reading program you reach a certain level and bog down. You don't seem able to move on and progress. The pacing drills will help you to work your way out of such slumps and get your reading program moving again.

Steps to Faster Reading

STEP 1: PREVIEW

When you read, do you start in with the first word, or do you look over the whole selection for a moment? Good readers preview the selection first—this helps to make them good, and fast, readers.

1. Read the Title. The first thing to do when previewing is to read the title of the selection. Titles are designed not only to announce the subject, but also to make the reader think. What can you learn from the title? What thoughts does it bring to mind? What do you already know about this subject?

2. Read the Opening Paragraph. If the first paragraph is long, read the first sentence or two instead. The first paragraph is the writer's opportunity to greet the reader. He may have something to tell you about what is to come. Some writers announce what they hope to tell you in the selection. Some writers tell why they are writing. Some writers just try to get the reader's attention—they may ask a provocative question.

3. Read the Closing Paragraph. If the last paragraph is long, read just the final line or two. The closing paragraph is the writer's last chance to talk to his reader. He may have something important to say at the end. Some writers repeat the main idea once more. Some writers draw a conclusion: this is what they have been leading up to. Some writers summarize their thoughts; they tie all the facts together.

4. Glance Through. Scan the selection quickly to see what else you can pick up. Discover whatever you can to help you read the selection. Are there names, dates, numbers? If so, you may have to read more slowly. Are there colorful adjectives? The selection might be light and fairly easy to read. Is the selection informative, containing a lot of facts, or conversational, an informal discussion with the reader?

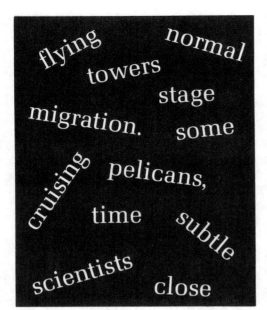

Steps to Faster Reading

STEP 2: READ FOR MEANING

When you read, do you just see words? Are you so occupied reading words that you sometimes fail to get the meaning? Good readers see beyond the words—they read for meaning. This makes them faster readers.

1. Build Concentration. You cannot read with understanding if you are not concentrating. Every reader's mind wanders occasionally; it is not a cause for alarm. When you discover that your thoughts have strayed, correct the situation right away. The longer you wait, the harder it becomes. Avoid distractions and distracting situations. Outside noises and activities will compete for your attention if you let them. Keep the preview information in mind as you read. This will help to focus your attention on the selection.

2. Read in Thought Groups. Individual words do not tell us much. They must be combined with other words in order to yield meaning. To obtain meaning from the printed page, therefore, the reader should see the words in meaningful combinations. If you see only a word at a time (called word-by-word reading), your comprehension suffers along with your speed. To improve both speed and comprehension, try to group the words into phrases which have a natural relationship to each other. For practice, you might want to read aloud, trying to speak the words in meaningful combinations.

3. Question the Author. To sustain the pace you have set for yourself, and to maintain a high level of comprehension, question the writer as you read. Continually ask yourself such questions as, "What does this mean? What is he saying now? How can I use this information?" Questions like these help you to concentrate fully on the selection.

Steps to Faster Reading

STEP 3: GRASP PARAGRAPH SENSE

The paragraph is the basic unit of meaning. If you can discover quickly and understand the main point of each paragraph, you can comprehend the author's message. Good readers know how to find the main ideas of paragraphs quickly. This helps to make them faster readers.

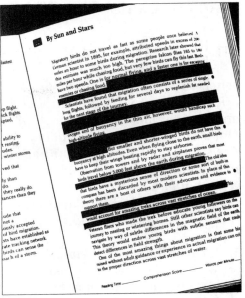

1. Find the Topic Sentence. The topic sentence, the sentence containing the main idea, is often the first sentence of a paragraph. It is followed by other sentences which support, develop, or explain the main idea. Sometimes a topic sentence comes at the end of a paragraph. When it does, the supporting details come first, building the base for the topic sentence. Some paragraphs do not have a topic sentence. Such paragraphs usually create a mood or feeling, rather than present information.

2. Understand Paragraph Structure. Every well-written paragraph has purpose. The purpose may be to inform, define, explain, persuade, compare or contrast, illustrate, and so on. The purpose should always relate to the main idea and expand on it. As you read each paragraph, see how the body of the paragraph is used to tell you more about the main idea or topic sentence. Read the supporting details intelligently, recognizing that what you are reading is all designed to develop the single main idea.

Steps to Faster Reading

STEP 4: ORGANIZE FACTS

When you read, do you tend to see a lot of facts without any apparent connection or relationship? Understanding how the facts all fit together to deliver the author's message is, after all, the reason for reading. Good readers organize facts as they read. This helps them to read rapidly and well.

1. Discover the Writer's Plan. Look for a clue or signal word early in the article which might reveal the author's structure. Every writer has a plan or outline which he follows. If the reader can discover his method of organization, he has the key to understanding the message. Sometimes the author gives you obvious signals. If he says, "There are three reasons . . ." the wise reader looks for a listing of the three items. Other less obvious signal words such as *moreover, otherwise, consequently* all tell the reader the direction the writer's message will take.

2. Relate as You Read. As you read the selection, keep the information learned during the preview in mind. See how the ideas you are reading all fit into place. Consciously strive to relate what you are reading to the title. See how the author is carrying through in his attempt to piece together a meaningful message. As you discover the relationship among the ideas, the message comes through quickly and clearly.

Timed
Reading
Selections

Stonehenge

For many centuries people have wondered about Stonehenge. They have studied the large circle of huge stone pillars. Some stones still stand erect. But others lie on the ground where they fell hundreds of years ago. Scientists have suggested that Stonehenge was a religious temple. Or, that it was a device to keep track of time.

The word Stonehenge means the "hanging stones," and it is an appropriate name. Some of the stone pillars still stand, just as they did 4,000 years ago. Across the tops of a few of the pillars, connecting to one another, are smaller stones that seem to "hang" in space.

Stonehenge stands on a rise in a rolling plain near Salisbury, England. The outer ring of stones at Stonehenge was made of 30 massive pillars. Some of them weigh up to 40 tons. These stones probably came from a quarry which is located 25 miles away. They had to be hauled over this distance by the people who built Stonehenge. They had to be cut into shape and set into place. After that, the smaller stones, called lintels, were set on top of them. Within the main ring of pillars at Stonehenge is another ring of smaller stones. These pillars weigh about 5 tons each. They are called bluestones because of their coloration. The closest quarry for stones like these is about 250 miles from the Salisbury Plain.

Stonehenge began as a large, circular ditch, built about 1900 B.C. This ditch is about 300 feet in diameter. As the people dug, they piled the soil along one rim and so a mound was made. Fifty-six holes inside the mound were probably dug at the same time.

Two hunded years later, the ring of bluestones was built. It was near the center of the ditch and mound. Only a few of these stones now stand; most have fallen over or have been removed. A broad avenue, now a slight depression in the land with mounds on either side, runs from Stonehenge across the Salisbury Plain. Some scientists think it was the main entrance and was built during this time period.

A hundred years or more went by before the large stone pillars were added, and their lintels set in place. Thus, at least 300 years were required to complete the "mystery" of Stonehenge.

Recalling Facts

1. Stonehenge may have functioned as a
   - ☐ a. fort.
   - ☐ b. temple.
   - ☐ c. village.

2. How many pillars made up the outer ring of stones?
   - ☐ a. 30
   - ☐ b. 15
   - ☐ c. 10

3. When was the first part of Stonehenge completed?
   - ☐ a. about 1600 B.C.
   - ☐ b. about 1900 A.D.
   - ☐ c. about 1900 B.C.

4. Name the type of stone that was used to build the inner ring of smaller pillars.
   - ☐ a. bluestone
   - ☐ b. granite
   - ☐ c. marble

5. What is an important part of Stonehenge besides the "hanging stones"?
   - ☐ a. a grove of trees
   - ☐ b. a ring-shaped ditch
   - ☐ c. a stone quarry

Understanding the Passage

6. From this selection we can conclude that
   - ☐ a. the purposes of Stonehenge are still not known.
   - ☐ b. Stonehenge was unimportant to its builders.
   - ☐ c. Stonehenge is no longer an object of curiosity.

7. Choose the best title for this article.
   - ☐ a. Different Types of Stone in Great Britain
   - ☐ b. A Mystery in Stone
   - ☐ c. Prehistoric People of Great Britain

8. Stonehenge was probably built
   - ☐ a. with iron tools.
   - ☐ b. by hundreds of people.
   - ☐ c. within a period of a few years.

9. Which ring of stones supports the lintels?
   - ☐ a. the outer ring
   - ☐ b. the inner ring
   - ☐ c. the third ring

10. What is another term for lintel?
    - ☐ a. pillar
    - ☐ b. column
    - ☐ c. "hanging stone"

What happens to all the solid waste produced in the United States? Well, some of it is thrown away. It litters streets, roadways, the countryside, and waterways. Some of it is burned in open air. Still some trash is left to sit in the open at garbage dumps. These dumps smell, look bad, and attract rats and insects. Some of the trash is buried. Valuable materials that might have been reused are thus lost. Some of the buried waste can be harmful. It leaks deadly chemicals which poison the land and the water.

Waste is everywhere. Each year we throw away more than 7 million television sets. We junk 7 million old cars and trucks. We use and discard 48 billion cans and 26 billion bottles. We toss out 30 million tons of paper. Waste disposal costs us four and a half billion dollars a year. Something has to be done with all this trash and garbage. Even though we are not sure of the best way to get rid of trash, we must make an effort.

Open garbage dumps are the most common places we put our solid wastes. Therefore, it's a good place to start. These dumps can be made better by turning them into clean landfills. In such a landfill, a layer of soil is applied daily over the waste. This helps to keep pests away and cuts down on the water pollutants that wash off in the rain. A landfill does away with the need to burn the waste, and this prevents wind-blown litter. When filled, the site can be planted with grass, shrubs, and trees and made into a park.

But ordinary sanitary landfills may not stop waste matter from seeping through the soil and ruining water supplies. Dangerous waste matter needs landfills that are sealed in a special way to stop seepage. In the past, harmful waste was burned. It was also dumped into waterways. But then pollution controls went into effect. More of these wastes showed up in landfills. The yearly amount of harmful waste is on the rise. Our health is threatened by the unsafe waste from these landfills.

There are good ways to get rid of the most dangerous waste without harming health or the ecology. But costs of such disposal are high. Federal and state governments are working with business firms and citizens to solve these cost and waste problems.

Reading Time _____ *Comprehension Score* _____ *Words per Minute* _____   17

Recalling Facts

1. Open dumps attract
   - ☐ a. game animals.
   - ☐ b. rats and insects.
   - ☐ c. trash collectors.

2. Some of the buried waste has deadly
   - ☐ a. chemicals.
   - ☐ b. insects.
   - ☐ c. plants.

3. How many junk cars and trucks are thrown away each year?
   - ☐ a. 7 million
   - ☐ b. 26 billion
   - ☐ c. 30 billion

4. Garbage dumps can be made better by turning them into
   - ☐ a. clean landfills.
   - ☐ b. parking lots.
   - ☐ c. usable canals.

5. The yearly amount of harmful waste is
   - ☐ a. decreasing.
   - ☐ b. increasing.
   - ☐ c. stable.

Understanding the Passage

6. Open garbage dumps are
   - ☐ a. beautiful.
   - ☐ b. dangerous.
   - ☐ c. restful.

7. We can see that many people
   - ☐ a. have open garbage dumps in their yards.
   - ☐ b. save millions of tons of newspapers.
   - ☐ c. throw away things that can be reused.

8. A clean landfill takes the place of
   - ☐ a. a beautiful park.
   - ☐ b. an open garbage dump.
   - ☐ c. an unpolluted waterway.

9. Getting rid of waste is
   - ☐ a. easy.
   - ☐ b. expensive.
   - ☐ c. unpopular.

10. This article hints that
    - ☐ a. litter along the highway is usually cleaned up by the town.
    - ☐ b. more and more people are concerned with waste disposal.
    - ☐ c. waste disposal is not an important problem.

The World of Folklore

Folklore is the customs, traditions, and beliefs that a group of people have passed on from generation to generation. They are usually passed on by the spoken word. In this way, folklore combines the dances, stories, arts and crafts, music, and religion of a culture.

Myths are the earliest types of folklore. Myths explain life and death. They explain the forces of nature. Myths are often related to religion. For example, we know that every star is a sun. People of long ago did not know what stars were. They made up myths to understand them. Every culture has its own stories to explain these twinkling lights. Ancient peoples told stories about changing seasons. The heroes of myths are usually gods and goddesses who act like humans but have unusual powers.

The fairy tale entertains and amuses. It takes place in a magical place where unusual things happen. All fairies have mystical powers. One popular fairy tale is *Cinderella*. She was a poor orphan who finally married a prince and lived "happily ever after." Cinderella had a fairy godmother who could change a pumpkin into a carriage. She did this just by waving her hand.

The fable shows people how they should live. Most fables tell stories about animals with human traits. They end with a moral. The best-known fables were collected by Aesop. He was a Greek slave who lived in the 5th century B.C. He did not write these fables, but he made them popular.

One popular fable is the story of the tortoise and the hare. The two animals had a race to see which was faster. The hare ran ahead of the tortoise and lay down for a rest. The tortoise plodded slowly by and won. The moral of this fable is simple. A person who works slowly and steadily will do more than one who works too quickly.

The legend, like the fable, also instructs. However, the legend is closer to life than the fable. It is sometimes based on a true story. Legends may tell about people who really lived and events that really occurred.

The stories of King Arthur and his Knights of the Round Table are legends. Many things have happened in these legends that can be traced to events in English history. But the story of Arthur is probably not true. There may have been a Merlin who actually lived. But can we believe that he really possessed magical powers?

Recalling Facts

1. What is the earliest type of folklore?
   - ☐ a. legend
   - ☐ b. myth
   - ☐ c. fairy tale

2. The fairy tale
   - ☐ a. entertains and amuses.
   - ☐ b. instructs.
   - ☐ c. records history.

3. The heroes of myths are
   - ☐ a. dragons.
   - ☐ b. fairies.
   - ☐ c. gods and goddesses.

4. Which of the following is closer to life?
   - ☐ a. a myth
   - ☐ b. a legend
   - ☐ c. a fairy tale

5. Cinderella was a
   - ☐ a. poor orphan girl.
   - ☐ b. fairy godmother.
   - ☐ c. historical person.

Understanding the Passage

6. Folklore seems to be present in
   - ☐ a. only western cultures.
   - ☐ b. all cultures of the world.
   - ☐ c. few cultures of the world.

7. Who collected the most famous fables?
   - ☐ a. Merlin.
   - ☐ b. Aesop.
   - ☐ c. Cinderella.

8. The stories of King Arthur and his Knights
   - ☐ a. cannot be traced in English history.
   - ☐ b. can be traced in French history.
   - ☐ c. can be traced in English history.

9. Explanations of the natural world are often told in
   - ☐ a. fairy tales.
   - ☐ b. legends.
   - ☐ c. myths.

10. A popular fable is the story of
    - ☐ a. a hare and a tortoise.
    - ☐ b. Cinderella.
    - ☐ c. King Arthur.

Blacksmith of the Gods

What are volcanoes? The word "volcano" comes from "Vulcan." This was the name of a Roman god. Centuries ago, people believed that Vulcan was the blacksmith of the gods. A volcano was the chimney of his forge. When clouds of dust billowed from the volcano and hot lava poured out, they thought Vulcan was at work. Vulcan made thunderbolts for Jupiter, king of the gods. He also made weapons for Mars, god of war. Today, of course, we know that volcanoes are part of nature. There's nothing magic about them.

Volcanoes are different from mountains. They are not made the way mountains are. They are made by the build-up of their own lava, ash, and dust. Most volcanoes are hills shaped like cones. These hills have formed around openings in the earth's surface. The openings are above pools of melted rock. These burning pools are found deep in the earth. At times, this liquid is forced up by gas pressure. When this happens, the melted rock breaks through weak places in the earth's crust. It pours from the opening as lava. It may even shoot into the air as thick clouds of lava dust. Pieces of lava fall back around the opening. Some of the finer dust may be blown away by the wind and fall to the ground many miles away.

The melted rock below the surface is known as "magma." After it is released from a volcano, it is called lava. It is red-hot when it first pours from the volcano. Then it slowly changes to dark red, gray, or black as it cools. Very hot lava glows like hot tar. Cool lava flows more slowly, like thick honey.

All lava that comes to the crust of the earth contains gas. The gas escapes easily from thin lava. But if the lava is thick and pasty, the gas escapes with explosive force. Gas in lava may be compared with the gas in a bottle of soda pop. Try an experiment. Put your thumb over the top of a soda bottle and shake it. You will see that the gas separates from the soda and forms bubbles. When you take your thumb away, there is a small explosion of gas and liquid. The gas in lava acts in somewhat the same way. It causes the terrible explosions that throw out great masses of solid rock as well as lava, dust, and ashes.

Recalling Facts

1. Long ago, people thought that Vulcan was a
   - ☐ a. blacksmith.
   - ☐ b. messenger.
   - ☐ c. warrior.

2. People thought that Vulcan made thunderbolts for
   - ☐ a. Jupiter.
   - ☐ b. Pluto.
   - ☐ c. Neptune.

3. Volcanoes are made of
   - ☐ a. iron and dust.
   - ☐ b. lava and ash.
   - ☐ c. sand and salt.

4. Most volcanoes are hills shaped like
   - ☐ a. cones.
   - ☐ b. saddles.
   - ☐ c. straws.

5. The melted rock below the earth's surface is known as
   - ☐ a. lava.
   - ☐ b. magma.
   - ☐ c. ore.

Understanding the Passage

6. We can see that the Romans
   - ☐ a. attacked Greece and killed her people.
   - ☐ b. often built cities near a volcano.
   - ☐ c. worshipped more than one god.

7. Volcanoes can be
   - ☐ a. harmful.
   - ☐ b. helpful.
   - ☐ c. useful.

8. The dust cloud from a volcano
   - ☐ a. can be seen at a distance.
   - ☐ b. is often filled with water.
   - ☐ c. usually settles near the volcano.

9. The magma or melted rock is very
   - ☐ a. hot.
   - ☐ b. soft.
   - ☐ c. sticky.

10. An exploding volcano is
    - ☐ a. calm.
    - ☐ b. noisy.
    - ☐ c. still.

5   Let It Fly

Bows and arrows are one of man's oldest weapons. Early man hunted with the bow more than 8,000 years ago. It was an important discovery for man. It gave him a deadly weapon with which he could kill his enemies. He could also kill prey from a distance.

The ordinary bow, or shortbow, was used by nearly all early people. This bow had limited power and a short range. However, man overcame these faults by learning to track his prey at close range. In fact, some African pygmies still hunt this way. They get very close to their prey, then shoot it with poisoned arrows. Even the American Indian rarely tried a shot past forty yards.

The longbow was most likely discovered when someone found out that a five-foot piece of wood made a better bow than a three-foot piece. The final length of the longbow was probably six feet, six inches. Hundreds of thousands of these bows were made and used for 300 years. However, not one is known to survive today. We believe that a force of about 100 pounds was needed to pull the string all the way back on a longbow. Anyone who used this bow had to be very strong.

The English longbow arrows were made of oak, ash, or birch. The arrows were usually feathered with wing feathers from the grey goose. The arrowheads were made of steel. They were broad and barbed. The archer carried twenty-four such arrows into battle. He could shoot one every five seconds if he had to. This made him a fearful enemy.

For a long time the bow was just a bent stick and a string. In fact, more changes have taken place in the bow and arrow in the past twenty-five years than in the last seven centuries. Today's bow is forceful. It is as exact as a gun. Plus, it requires little strength to draw the string. Modern bows also have fine sights. An expert can hit a bull's-eye many times in a row from a good distance away. In indoor contests, perfect scores from forty yards are common. Matches have been lost when a winning arrow was stopped by one already in the bull's-eye.

The invention of the bow itself ranks with the discovery of fire and the wheel. It was a great step forward for man.

Recalling Facts

1. Bows and arrows are one of man's oldest
   - ☐ a. charms.
   - ☐ b. toys.
   - ☐ c. weapons.

2. The bow was used more than
   - ☐ a. 8,000 years ago.
   - ☐ b. 20,000 years ago.
   - ☐ c. 30,000 years ago.

3. The shortbow had limited
   - ☐ a. length.
   - ☐ b. power.
   - ☐ c. use.

4. Anyone who used the longbow had to be
   - ☐ a. fat.
   - ☐ b. strong.
   - ☐ c. tall.

5. The arrowheads on a longbow were made of
   - ☐ a. feathers.
   - ☐ b. steel.
   - ☐ c. wood.

Understanding the Passage

6. Early man used the bow and arrow to
   - ☐ a. defend himself.
   - ☐ b. keep warm.
   - ☐ c. plant crops.

7. Man tracked his prey when he used the shortbow because the shortbow did not
   - ☐ a. bend easily.
   - ☐ b. shoot far.
   - ☐ c. weigh much.

8. When at close range, early man used
   - ☐ a. the shortbow.
   - ☐ b. the longbow.
   - ☐ c. rocks.

9. The longbow was probably discovered
   - ☐ a. before the shortbow.
   - ☐ b. at the same time as the shortbow.
   - ☐ c. after the shortbow.

10. Today's bows are very
    - ☐ a. accurate.
    - ☐ b. colorful.
    - ☐ c. heavy.

6 A Good Experience

In one sense, an allowance is a child's share of the family income. It can be a good experience that parents can provide for their children. The amount should be what the family can afford. It should be given to the youngster to do with as she pleases. It should not be used as a tool to win the youngster's good behavior.

An allowance is not a bribe. It should be thought of as a learning tool. It can give a youngster firsthand experience in learning how to spend money. It can teach her how to get the best value for what she buys. It can help her use her skills in arithmetic.

Many youngsters make mistakes and buy unwisely at first. Some rush out to spend all their money the moment they get it. They forget that once it is spent, there will be no more for several days. From such haste, youngsters can learn how to choose wisely and spend carefully.

Parents need to know when to begin to give an allowance. They also want to decide how much to give. When a youngster starts school, she may want an allowance. She may have friends who receive one. A good time for considering an allowance may be when a youngster makes daily requests for ice cream or candy. This will help her to see the value of money.

At first a youngster may receive only half an allowance but get it twice a week. This would be a help to someone who finds a full week too long. A youngster will soon figure out that she can have two candy bars this week, or she can save her allowance for two weeks and buy a toy. She learns that she cannot have both the candy and the toy.

A wise parent will not control her child's buying. If a child makes her own mistakes with her own money, she is more apt to learn from her mistakes. Also, a child should not be made to save a part of each week's allowance. An allowance should not be taken away as punishment for bad behavior. An allowance should not be thought of as pay for doing household chores.

A youngster should be encouraged to be generous. An allowance should help her see that money isn't everything. No amount of money can buy friendship. Things such as love and respect do not have a price tag.

Recalling Facts

1. An allowance gives a child a chance to share in the family's
   - ☐ a. chores.
   - ☐ b. meals.
   - ☐ c. income.

2. The amount of an allowance should depend upon what the family can
   - ☐ a. afford.
   - ☐ b. borrow.
   - ☐ c. inherit.

3. An allowance can give a child the chance to use her
   - ☐ a. arithmetic skills.
   - ☐ b. map skills.
   - ☐ c. reading skills.

4. An allowance should be given once or twice a
   - ☐ a. week.
   - ☐ b. month.
   - ☐ c. year.

5. An allowance should not be used as a tool to win a child's
   - ☐ a. friends.
   - ☐ b. good behavior.
   - ☐ c. self-respect.

Understanding the Passage

6. Parents should give an allowance to
   - ☐ a. make the child behave.
   - ☐ b. pay a child for chores.
   - ☐ c. teach the value of money.

7. We can see that children learn the value of money by
   - ☐ a. listening to friends.
   - ☐ b. making mistakes.
   - ☐ c. visiting the bank.

8. At first, most youngsters spend their money
   - ☐ a. foolishly.
   - ☐ b. carefully.
   - ☐ c. wisely.

9. An allowance should encourage a youngster to be
   - ☐ a. bold.
   - ☐ b. stingy.
   - ☐ c. unselfish.

10. This passage hints that giving the child an allowance
    - ☐ a. can be harmful to the child.
    - ☐ b. is a good experience for the child.
    - ☐ c. takes away the child's self-respect.

Castles in the Air

Life during the Middle Ages was hard. People were always at war. Therefore, castles were built to protect people from their enemies.

The castle was the home of a lord and his family. It was also the home of the soldiers. The soldiers were there to protect the castle, the lord, and his family. They also protected the village from attack. The castle was also the prison and the treasure house. It was even the center of local government.

Most castles were built on a hill or high ground. This made the castle easy to defend. A moat (a deep ditch filled with water) was built around the castle. A drawbridge, which could be raised and lowered with winches and chains, lay across the moat.

During the Middle Ages, most castles were built in the shape of a square. They had a large tower in each corner. These towers were usually made of stone. A thick stone wall ran from tower to tower and formed an area called the inner ward. A large central tower was called the keep. This was always the strongest part of the castle. The lord and his family lived on the upper floors of the keep. The soldiers lived on the lower levels. The keep had many secret rooms and getaway passages. It was here, in the keep, that all the village people would hide during times of great danger. There were many underground tunnels leading to the keep. The other towers were used for the prison. The great hall was the place used for town meetings. The kitchen and bake shop were also part of the castle.

The space outside the towers and wall was called the outer ward. This outer ward was surrounded by another wall. This second wall also ran around the whole village. The top of this wall had a walk for the soldiers and battlements (high stone shields). From behind the battlements, the soldiers could hide to shoot their arrows and cast stones at the enemy.

At the end of the Middle Ages, castles disappeared. They were replaced by forts. But many rich homes, homes of lords and earls, were still built in the shape of a castle. Castles have always held the interest of people. Even today in European countries the old romantic castles are a big tourist attraction. Many people flock to see these ancient buildings.

Recalling Facts

1. Castles were used to protect people from their
   □ a. enemies.
   □ b. friends.
   □ c. pets.

2. The castle was also a
   □ a. church.
   □ b. market.
   □ c. prison.

3. Most castles were built on a
   □ a. cliff.
   □ b. hill.
   □ c. lake.

4. The ditch filled with water that surrounded the castle was called a
   □ a. crevice.
   □ b. keep.
   □ c. moat.

5. Battlements are stone
   □ a. shields.
   □ b. statues.
   □ c. towers.

Understanding the Passage

6. People during the Middle Ages were
   □ a. friendly.
   □ b. poetic.
   □ c. warlike.

7. We can see that castles were
   □ a. small shacks.
   □ b. sturdy buildings.
   □ c. tiny caves.

8. If a friend wished to enter the castle, the drawbridge had to be
   □ a. destroyed.
   □ b. lowered.
   □ c. raised.

9. This article hints that castles were mostly made of
   □ a. stone.
   □ b. straw.
   □ c. wood.

10. Getaway passages were probably used when people wanted to
   □ a. escape.
   □ b. fight.
   □ c. vacation.

Wood decay is caused by small plants called fungi. These plants cannot live on wood that has a moisture content of less than about 30 percent. The wood in most well-built homes is safe because the moisture content is rarely above 15 percent. The way to stop decay is simple. Keep wood dry.

Keeping wood dry is not always that easy to do. The outside walls of a house are open to rain that blows against them. Soil carries water. It can wet any wood that touches it. Also, if there are plumbing leaks in your home, the inside wood can get wet.

Wood must be kept dry at all times because wood soaks up water and holds it for a long time. From time to time, heavy rains can supply enough water for decay to begin.

If you know that wood will become wet, it can be protected. Wood can be treated with preservatives. For long term safety, the preservative should be put on under pressure. If the wood comes in touch with the ground, only pressure treatment will do the job. Some pieces of wood that only get wet from time to time can be treated to stop decay by brushing on a preservative. The correct chemical to use for treatment depends upon what the wood is used for. Some chemicals give off a terrible smell. These are not good for use indoors. Others cause paint to peel. You should mention what the wood is used for when you buy the preservative.

Mold and stain fungi can attack wood. Molds grow mainly on the surface but may get inside the outer sapwood. The dark color caused by mold on wood can be removed by light sanding. Stain fungi go beyond the outer layers and cause a dark color that cannot be removed. Both molds and stain feed on wood. By themselves, they do not decay or weaken the wood. But, they do increase the wood's ability to take on and hold moisture. Thus, they increase the possibility of future decay. If you see signs of molds and stain fungi, you may have a problem.

Wood decays slowly at temperatures below 40 degrees Farenheit. So, decay is more rapid in the South than in the North. Decay is also more rapid in humid than in dry regions, even though the plants that cause decay are present everywhere throughout the United States.

Reading Time _____   *Comprehension Score* _____   *Words per Minute* _____   29

Recalling Facts

1. Wood decay is caused by small plants called
   - ☐ a. algae.
   - ☐ b. fungi.
   - ☐ c. germs.

2. In order to live, wood decaying plants need a moisture content of
   - ☐ a. 15 percent or less.
   - ☐ b. 25 percent.
   - ☐ c. 30 percent or more.

3. The wood in most well-built homes has a moisture content which is rarely above
   - ☐ a. 15 percent.
   - ☐ b. 30 percent.
   - ☐ c. 65 percent.

4. Which of the following is a good carrier of water?
   - ☐ a. cloth
   - ☐ b. iron
   - ☐ c. soil

5. Wood can be protected from decay by using
   - ☐ a. cement.
   - ☐ b. preservatives.
   - ☐ c. water.

Understanding the Passage

6. Wood-decaying plants live well in wood that is
   - ☐ a. dry.
   - ☐ b. smooth.
   - ☐ c. wet.

7. The outside walls are constantly in contact with
   - ☐ a. insects.
   - ☐ b. moisture.
   - ☐ c. plants.

8. The best way to keep wood from decaying is to
   - ☐ a. keep it dry.
   - ☐ b. sand it.
   - ☐ c. split it.

9. Molds can cause wood to
   - ☐ a. bend and snap.
   - ☐ b. change color.
   - ☐ c. splinter easily.

10. The possibility of wood decay is high in the southern United States because of the
    - ☐ a. higher temperatures.
    - ☐ b. many rivers.
    - ☐ c. salt water.

9   Life of a President

Our sixteenth president was Abraham Lincoln. He was born in a log cabin in Kentucky on February 12, 1809. Abe did not have an easy life. When he was nine years old, his mother died.

At the age of 21, Abe set out for Illinois. He worked at many jobs. He split rails for fences. He worked as a clerk in a store. He served as a village postmaster. Because Abe had to work, he could not always go to school. In fact, Abe had very little schooling. Even so, he did much reading and studying during his spare time. By 1837, he had passed the examination to practice law. His self-education had paid off.

At that time, Lincoln moved to Springfield, the capital of Illinois. As a lawyer and politician, he became well known throughout the state. When he was 37 years old, he was elected to the United States House of Representatives. Later, when he returned from Washington, he helped organize the new Republican Party. In 1858, Lincoln became a candidate for the U.S. Senate. He took part in several famous debates with Stephen A. Douglas, the other candidate. Lincoln lost the election, but he became famous. His fame spread throughout the country.

In 1860, Lincoln was asked to run for President by the Republican Party. As a candidate, he promised two things. He promised to hold the states together. He promised to stop the spread of slavery in the country. Lincoln won the election. But he was not able to keep his promises without bloodshed. His term of office was not a peaceful one.

Just as he was elected, the Southern states began to leave the union. Soon, war broke out between the North and the South. Abe was elected for a second term a few months before the War between the States ended. In 1865, a heartbroken President saw the war finally come to a close.

Abe wanted all the people to help rebuild our land. He also wanted them to keep it free. He hoped the states could be joined once more.

However, Abe didn't see his dreams come true. On April 14, 1865, he attended the Ford Theatre in Washington. There, Lincoln was shot by John Wilkes Booth, an actor. The next morning Lincoln died. The whole nation mourned the passing of one of the greatest leaders history has ever known.

Recalling Facts

1. Abraham Lincoln was born in
   - ☐ a. Kentucky.
   - ☐ b. Louisiana.
   - ☐ c. Mississippi.

2. Abe's mother died when he was
   - ☐ a. five.
   - ☐ b. seven.
   - ☐ c. nine.

3. In 1837, Abe passed the test to practice
   - ☐ a. law.
   - ☐ b. medicine.
   - ☐ c. religion.

4. The War between the States ended in
   - ☐ a. 1809.
   - ☐ b. 1860.
   - ☐ c. 1865.

5. Lincoln was killed by
   - ☐ a. Benedict Arnold.
   - ☐ b. John Wilkes Booth.
   - ☐ c. Stephen A. Douglas.

Understanding the Passage

6. This article hints that Lincoln's parents were not
   - ☐ a. happy.
   - ☐ b. kind.
   - ☐ c. rich.

7. Which political party did Lincoln belong to?
   - ☐ a. Democratic
   - ☐ b. Republican
   - ☐ c. Socialist

8. We can see that in 1858
   - ☐ a. Lincoln became President.
   - ☐ b. Stephen Douglas became a senator.
   - ☐ c. war broke out between the states.

9. We can conclude from this article that Lincoln
   - ☐ a. could not stop the War between the States.
   - ☐ b. fought in the War between the States.
   - ☐ c. wanted the War between the States.

10. Lincoln died during his
    - ☐ a. first term in office.
    - ☐ b. second term in office.
    - ☐ c. third term in office.

Planting a tree correctly will help the new tree you plant live and grow properly. There are some guides for proper tree planting.

One thing you should do is to plant at the right time of the year. Some trees should be planted in the early spring; some in the fall. The best time depends on the kind of tree you are going to put in the ground. If there is a label on the tree, it will have this information. Or, you can ask the salesperson at the nursery.

Be sure, too, that the hole you dig is big enough. If your tree has bare roots, the hole must be deep and wide enough for them to fit without cramping. Some trees are sold with a ball of burlap around the roots. Holes for these trees should be at least 12 inches wider than the diameter of the ball. If plastic has been used to wrap the roots, remove it before planting. A burlap wrap only needs to be loosened after the tree is in the ground. Before planting, protect the tree roots from drying. Keep the tree and roots away from the sun and wind.

After placing the tree in the hole, spread the roots out evenly. Be careful not to damage them. Tamp and water the soil with care around the roots.

Water the tree right after planting. Keep on watering the tree at regular periods for the next two years. Water heavily near the roots about once a week for several hours during the growing season. Continue this well into the fall. The soil should be soaked, but not flooded.

Do not fertilize the tree at planting time. If you do, you may burn the roots. Whether to fertilize and when to fertilize depends again on the type of tree. Other things to keep in mind are the kind of soil and the time of year.

When planting trees more than three feet tall, other things must be considered. The tree will have to be supported until the roots have taken. Connect the tree to poles using rubber-wrapped wires. You will need to support the new tree for one or two years. Also, the bark on new trees is tender. You may need to protect the bare trunk with burlap. Keep animals away from the tree. Put up a fence with chicken wire to prevent animal damage.

Recalling Facts

1. When you plant a tree, make sure you plant it at the right time of the
   - ☐ a. day.
   - ☐ b. week.
   - ☐ c. year.

2. Before planting, protect the tree roots from the
   - ☐ a. dew.
   - ☐ b. rain.
   - ☐ c. sun.

3. When you place the tree in the hole, you should
   - ☐ a. fill the hole with water.
   - ☐ b. pack rocks in the hole.
   - ☐ c. spread out the roots.

4. After you plant your tree, you should water it at regular times for two
   - ☐ a. days.
   - ☐ b. months.
   - ☐ c. years.

5. If you fertilize the tree at planting time, you may
   - ☐ a. burn the roots.
   - ☐ b. damage the bark.
   - ☐ c. strip the leaves.

Understanding the Passage

6. This article tells us how to
   - ☐ a. choose a tree.
   - ☐ b. cut down a tree.
   - ☐ c. plant a tree.

7. If you plant a tree at the wrong time, it might
   - ☐ a. bloom.
   - ☐ b. die.
   - ☐ c. wilt.

8. When you plant your tree, you must be careful not to damage the
   - ☐ a. bark.
   - ☐ b. leaves.
   - ☐ c. roots.

9. Newly planted trees need a lot of
   - ☐ a. fertilizer.
   - ☐ b. water.
   - ☐ c. wind.

10. This article hints that a newly planted six-foot tree must be
    - ☐ a. sprayed.
    - ☐ b. supported.
    - ☐ c. trimmed.

Do you plan to visit Italy someday? If so, it's a good idea to know about the country and its people. Italy has two very different areas. The business centers and large cities of the North hum with noise. The South, on the other hand, enjoys the sleepy charm of the country. People of the North like the bustle of city life. They enjoy all the things a city has to offer. Those from the South like a slower pace. They like their rural surroundings. One thing all Italians have in common is their zest for life.

The climate of Italy is like that of California. It is sunny and warm all year in the South. Except in the mountains, summers are warm all over the country. Winter brings snow, sleet, cold rain, and fog to the North. Central Italy is mild in winter.

Many Italians are happiest when in groups. Wherever they gather, you are likely to hear fine singing and happy laughter.

A building boom is going on in the cities of Italy. Steel and glass skyscrapers tower over ancient ruins. Italy throbs with life and color. Talk on the street corners is lively. The background music coming from open windows could be classical or the latest hit tune. Donkeys and street peddlers sometimes add to the color and noise.

The city streets are busy. Here you will see well-dressed people. These people are going to work in new office buildings. The street traffic includes different kinds of cars. You can even spot some motor scooters and bicycles.

Italians also like food. They are good cooks. Each city and region has its own specialties. Bologna, for instance, is known for its sausages. Olive oil, garlic, and tomatoes are used more freely in cooking in the South than in the North. Some Northerners use butter instead of olive oil. You will see rice on their plates instead of pasta.

An Italian dinner begins with appetizers and ends many courses later with a fine dessert. In the course of a dinner, you can sample some of Italy's fine cheeses. There are many to choose from. There are also many fine wines, and they are reasonably priced.

You may never visit Italy. Still, it's nice to read about its lively and colorful personality. Maybe someday you will be lucky enough to see part of this wonderful land.

Recalling Facts

1. The business areas of Italy are found in the
   - ☐ a. East.
   - ☐ b. North.
   - ☐ c. South.

2. Italians who live in the city enjoy
   - ☐ a. a faster pace.
   - ☐ b. a slower pace.
   - ☐ c. better food.

3. The climate of Italy is like that of
   - ☐ a. California.
   - ☐ b. Mississippi.
   - ☐ c. New York.

4. Central Italy is mild during the
   - ☐ a. spring.
   - ☐ b. summer.
   - ☐ c. winter.

5. Which of the following adds to the color and noise of Italy?
   - ☐ a. roving circuses
   - ☐ b. street peddlers
   - ☐ c. wildlife

Understanding the Passage

6. The life-styles of Northern and Southern Italy are
   - ☐ a. exactly the same.
   - ☐ b. quite similar.
   - ☐ c. very different.

7. The southern part of Italy is mostly
   - ☐ a. country.
   - ☐ b. desert.
   - ☐ c. swamp.

8. Southern Italy has warmer weather than
   - ☐ a. Sicily.
   - ☐ b. Eastern Italy.
   - ☐ c. Northern Italy.

9. To most Italians, dinner should be
   - ☐ a. long and luscious.
   - ☐ b. short and sweet.
   - ☐ c. simple and serious.

10. Italian streets are
    - ☐ a. dangerous.
    - ☐ b. noisy.
    - ☐ c. quiet.

12 The Romantic Center

Fireplaces tend to affect people in a strange way. They seem to have a romance all their own. Well, they should. Fireplaces were once the center of family life. When the West was being settled, the fireplace was the only energy source in the home. It provided heat, light, and cooking facilities. We have all heard the tale of Abe Lincoln being born in a log cabin. He is said to have studied his law books in front of the open fire. He did his writing on the back of the fireplace shovel.

In large Colonial homes, there were a number of fireplaces. There would be one in the living room and another in the library. Often, there would be a fireplace in each bedroom. People burned logs in the open fireplace because logs were the only fuel that was around. Later, modern fireplaces burned "gas logs." These were artificial logs that were really gas outlets. Many of these are still around today.

As homes began to be built with heating furnaces, fireplaces started to disappear. While a few homes still had them, they were more for show than anything else. In fact, some of the fireplaces in today's homes are not really fireplaces at all. That is, they do not have hearths or chimneys or dampers or other things that a fireplace needs. It would be quite dangerous to build a real fire in one of these.

But today, fireplaces have begun to make a strong comeback. Part of this is due to the high cost of fuel and energy. People are using them more and more. With this new use, there is a need for people to learn the rules of fireplace safety.

There are some things we should all know about open fires in the home. For example, did you know that sparks can leap from an open fire? These sparks can ignite anything in the room that will burn. This is why a screen made of wire or special glass should be placed across the fireplace.

If charcoal is burned in a poorly vented fireplace, deadly gases could be released into the room. Logs you buy at the store are made of sawdust and wax. These should be handled differently from natural logs. They should be burned one at a time and not stacked.

Recalling Facts

1. Fireplaces were once the center of
   - ☐ a. early education.
   - ☐ b. family life.
   - ☐ c. social gatherings.

2. Later on in time, modern fireplaces burned
   - ☐ a. dried leaves.
   - ☐ b. gas logs.
   - ☐ c. seasoned wood.

3. Today, fireplaces have made a strong comeback because of the high cost of
   - ☐ a. fuel.
   - ☐ b. groceries.
   - ☐ c. houses.

4. Charcoal can be a dangerous fuel because it
   - ☐ a. does not burn.
   - ☐ b. shoots off sparks.
   - ☐ c. gives off deadly gases.

5. Logs you buy in the store are made of
   - ☐ a. charcoal and wood.
   - ☐ b. newspaper and oil.
   - ☐ c. sawdust and wax.

Understanding the Passage

6. Fireplaces were
   - ☐ a. important to the colonists.
   - ☐ b. invented by the English.
   - ☐ c. never used in Europe.

7. It was usual for a large Colonial house to
   - ☐ a. be built with one central fireplace.
   - ☐ b. have fireplaces for heating.
   - ☐ c. have a wood-burning stove.

8. Some of the fireplaces in today's homes are used for
   - ☐ a. cooking.
   - ☐ b. decoration.
   - ☐ c. storage.

9. Why is it good to use a fireplace screen?
   - ☐ a. It adds decoration to the fireplace.
   - ☐ b. It holds the logs in their proper place.
   - ☐ c. It prevents sparks from leaving the fireplace.

10. If not used properly, a fireplace can be
    - ☐ a. dangerous.
    - ☐ b. sturdy.
    - ☐ c. untidy.

The theater of the Orient is very different from that of the western world. An American watching a Chinese play for the first time would not understand it. The language and the symbolism that make up a good part of the action are very different.

There is little scenery, but the costumes are of lovely brocades and silks. The actors' faces are painted with the color that indicates their character. Women sometimes play men's roles and men play women's.

One person that is seldom seen on a western stage is always on view on a Chinese stage. He or she is the property person. This person moves chairs, hands out swords and fans, and changes props. This person, dressed all in black, is meant to seem invisible.

Traditional Chinese plays begin at noon and go on for six to seven hours. The play-goers move around, sip tea, and chat with friends. Meanwhile, they keep up with what is going on on the stage. They are probably not watching one play, but parts of different plays. This would seem quite strange to a western audience.

The Chinese theater was intended for the pleasure of the aristocracy. These plays have been staged in the same way for centuries. They use the same conventions and symbols. But the uneducated Chinese do not understand much of the symbolism.

The Japanese have a traditional theater that produces Noh plays. These are the classic plays of the nobility. Noh actors wear masks and men play all of the roles. The only scenery is a painted pine tree. There is space for a chorus of men on one side of the stage. Musicians and property persons sit to the rear. All the action is formal, symbolic, and difficult to follow. The plays are about religious and historic subjects, usually tragic.

The popular theater of Japan is called the Kabuki. It began in the 17th century and consists of plays that are concerned with material from common life and history. Between plays, there is singing, dancing, and dramatic dialogue.

Bunraku is the doll theater of Japan. It has been in existence much longer than Kabuki. The puppets are three or more feet tall. It takes three people to operate one. The chief handler operates the head and right arm. An assistant operates the left arm. Another assistant operates the feet. The assistants are dressed in black and are also "invisible" to the Japanese audience.

Recalling Facts

1. In traditional Chinese theater there is
   □ a. little scenery.
   □ b. only a painted pine tree.
   □ c. much scenery.

2. Noh plays are a form of
   □ a. Chinese theater.
   □ b. puppet theater.
   □ c. Japanese theater.

3. What is the popular theater of Japan?
   □ a. Noh plays
   □ b. the Kabuki
   □ c. the Bunraku

4. Chinese plays last
   □ a. six to seven hours.
   □ b. one hour.
   □ c. four hours.

5. Women are not permitted to act in
   □ a. Chinese theater.
   □ b. Noh plays.
   □ c. Kabuki theater.

Understanding the Passage

6. What is a similarity between Bunraku and western puppet shows?
   □ a. the language and the symbolism
   □ b. the costumes
   □ c. the use of dolls or puppets

7. Who is considered "invisible" in Chinese theater?
   □ a. the property person
   □ b. the actors
   □ c. the musicians

8. The audience at a Chinese play
   □ a. sits quietly.
   □ b. moves around and sips tea.
   □ c. ignores the action on stage.

9. In Chinese plays, the actors' faces are painted to
   □ a. show respect for their audience.
   □ b. hide their features.
   □ c. indicate their character.

10. How many people does it take to operate one Japanese puppet?
    □ a. one
    □ b. two
    □ c. three

Two Famous Rivers of the World

The Nile has been a river shrouded in romance since ancient times. It is still this way for many tourists who visit each year. Thousands of years ago, an early people built the Sphinx and the early pyramids in Egypt. Papyrus grows along the banks of the Nile. From this reed the first paper was made. Many great cities once stood along the Nile. Cairo, near the pyramids, has become the largest city in Africa. Memphis, the ancient capital of Egypt, is now a village.

The Nile is 4,000 miles long and begins in two branches: the Blue Nile and the White Nile. For many years, the Nile's source was a mystery. Then, explorers traced the Blue Nile to the mountains of Ethiopia. They traced the White Nile to the lake region in tropical Africa. The two Niles meet at Khartoum in Sudan. There the river flows through the world's largest deserts. It rushes over a series of cataracts until it comes to the Egyptian delta.

People have tried to control the Nile's floods for 4,000 years. Heavy rains in Ethiopia cause the waters to rise in the fall to thirty feet above their springtime level. Today, modern dams like the Aswan hold back the floods and irrigate the land. Still, much irrigation is done with water wheels of ancient design, often turned by animals.

There are few railroads in China, and the commerce of this nation depends on the great rivers. For centuries, the Yangtze has been a great artery of travel. The junks, or riverboats, move slowly along the river as they have for thousands of years. Many of these boats have a large eye painted on the prow. This is so they can "see" their way. Thousands of Chinese make their homes on these junks. They often spend their whole lives on the Yangzte.

The Yangzte's source is in Tibet. It flows for 3,500 miles through some of the most beautiful mountains in the world. In its middle course, it flows to Chungking through a province as large as France. Below this province, the river has eroded its way through gorges.

In its last descent to the China Sea, the Yangtze travels wide plains. Its water is important for irrigation. Sometimes, entire families tread wheels to raise the water from the river for crops. After great rains, the Yangtze overflows and covers large areas of farmland. This destroys farmland and can cause famine.

Recalling Facts

1. The Nile is
   - ☐ a. 3,500 miles long.
   - ☐ b. 1,000 miles long.
   - ☐ c. 4,000 miles long.

2. What are the Blue Nile and the White Nile?
   - ☐ a. branches of the Nile
   - ☐ b. Egyptian villages
   - ☐ c. Egyptian deltas

3. One of the monuments in ancient Egypt is the
   - ☐ a. papyrus.
   - ☐ b. Sphinx.
   - ☐ c. Yangzte.

4. The Yangzte's source is in
   - ☐ a. China.
   - ☐ b. Chungking province.
   - ☐ c. Tibet.

5. Commercial travel on the Yangzte often takes the place of
   - ☐ a. railroad travel.
   - ☐ b. automobile travel.
   - ☐ c. airplane travel.

Understanding the Passage

6. The Yangzte and the Nile are the names of two
   - ☐ a. important rivers.
   - ☐ b. countries.
   - ☐ c. Egyptian pyramids.

7. Junks are painted with an eye on their prow to
   - ☐ a. identify them to their owners.
   - ☐ b. allow them to "see."
   - ☐ c. make them more attractive.

8. What is a good title for this selection?
   - ☐ a. River Roads of China and Egypt
   - ☐ b. The Pyramids and the Sphinx of Egypt
   - ☐ c. Irrigation and Flood Control

9. Junks are the
   - ☐ a. names of Chinese villages.
   - ☐ b. riverboat homes of Chinese families.
   - ☐ c. branches of the Yangzte.

10. The source of the Blue Nile is the
    - ☐ a. Nile Delta.
    - ☐ b. Egyptian deserts.
    - ☐ c. mountains of Ethiopia.

15   Satisfaction Guaranteed

It may take some time and effort to find the lawyer who will be just right for you. It is wise to search for a family lawyer who can advise you about things before they happen. This way you can take your time. If you wait until you are in a jam, you may have to make a mad dash to find someone to represent you. You may not make the best choice if you are under pressure. Time spent selecting a lawyer is time well spent. The satisfaction you will get from having made the right choice will make the search time all worthwhile.

One way to find a lawyer is to look for a satisfied client. Talk to your family and friends. See if they have used a lawyer whose services pleased them. Find out, too, what sort of matter the lawyer handled for them. Lawyers tend to specialize in a certain branch of the law. A lawyer may not want to handle a matter outside of her specialty.

Check to see if there is a lawyer referral service where you live. Such a service is often sponsored by the local bar association. If there is one, you will find it listed in the phone book. When you call, the service will give you the name of an attorney. Have a first interview with her for a stated fee. It should be a modest fee. At the meeting, you can find out if you need further legal aid.

There may not be a referral service where you live. But there should be a local bar association. If so, you should find it listed in the phone book. Or you can ask at the county courthouse. Someone there will know the name of the president of the bar association and her address. You can then ask her for the name of a good lawyer. Make it clear that you are asking her as president of the bar association for her opinion. Tell her the kind of service you are seeking.

If you can't afford to pay a fee, you can still get legal help. There may be a legal aid society where you live. Or there may be a group of lawyers who give free legal advice in certain cases. You can find out by looking in the phone book or by asking at the courthouse.

Recalling Facts

1. Finding the right lawyer takes
   - ☐ a. education and experience.
   - ☐ b. money and patience.
   - ☐ c. time and effort.

2. One good way to find a lawyer is to look for a
   - ☐ a. library.
   - ☐ b. police station.
   - ☐ c. satisfied client.

3. Lawyers tend to specialize in a certain branch of
   - ☐ a. law.
   - ☐ b. medicine.
   - ☐ c. politics.

4. A lawyer referral service is often sponsored by the local
   - ☐ a. aid association.
   - ☐ b. bar association.
   - ☐ c. court association.

5. Lawyer referral services may be listed in the
   - ☐ a. dictionary.
   - ☐ b. farmer's almanac.
   - ☐ c. phone book.

Understanding the Passage

6. What would be a good title for this passage?
   - ☐ a. Famous Law Schools
   - ☐ b. How to Choose a Lawyer
   - ☐ c. History of Law

7. A good lawyer
   - ☐ a. gives free advice.
   - ☐ b. has few clients.
   - ☐ c. may be hard to find.

8. This passage hints that there are
   - ☐ a. few lawyers.
   - ☐ b. many branches of law.
   - ☐ c. not enough law schools.

9. Which of the following may give free legal advice?
   - ☐ a. the lawyer referral service
   - ☐ b. the legal aid society
   - ☐ c. the local bar association

10. We can see that
    - ☐ a. lawyers are only found in large cities.
    - ☐ b. poor people may get free legal advice.
    - ☐ c. the legal aid society charges a high fee.

16   The Eruption of Mount Saint Helens

On May 18, 1980, Mount Saint Helens in Washington erupted. A huge blast blew away more than 1,000 feet of the mountain. It also killed at least 34 people. The eruption rained mud in the immediate area. It rained ash over many states. It changed the environment for many years to come. And it clearly showed the force of nature.

The blast was heard 135 miles away from the volcano. It equaled the force of 10 million tons of TNT! In comparison, it was 500 times as strong as the atomic bomb dropped on Hiroshima, Japan, in 1945. All life in an area of 155 square miles was destroyed by the eruption. Large trees were felled within 15 miles of the summit. Waterways were clogged with debris, causing $2.7 billion in damage.

Mount Saint Helens had been inactive from 1857 to March 27, 1980. Then, it began to shake with local earthquakes. The 1980 eruptions were the first in the United States outside of Alaska for some years. Back in 1921, Lassen Peak in California erupted. As an active volcano, Mount Saint Helens has small eruptions even now.

A volcano like Mount Saint Helens is an opening in the earth. Ashes, hot gases, and rock burst from the volcano when magma builds up. Magma is melted rock found beneath the earth's surface. This magma gathers near the surface. Here it is under great pressure. Soon it erupts, spouting a "rain" of hot material.

Most volcanoes are found in the Ring of Fire which "rings" the Pacific Ocean. The earth's outer shell is divided into 20 large plates that slide over rock. This rock is partially melted. Most volcanoes form when two plates clash and one slides under the other. The edges and lower plates melt because of great friction. The melted material forms a peak or a volcano.

Scientists predict that the recovery of wildlife around Mount Saint Helens will take many years. Large animals, such as deer, will not return soon because they need tree cover. Most of the forest cover was destroyed by the eruption. Smaller animals have returned to the area. But they need insects for food. Insects must adapt to a changed plant setting of fewer, younger plants. Millions of fish were killed by the hot mud that blocked the rivers. Many of the spawning grounds were also destroyed by the mud from this volcano.

---

*Reading Time*_____   *Comprehension Score*_____   *Words per Minute*_____   **45**

Recalling Facts

1. Mount Saint Helens is located in the state of
   - □ a. Washington.
   - □ b. Massachusetts.
   - □ c. Florida.

2. The blast of the eruption of Mount Saint Helens was heard
   - □ a. 300 miles away.
   - □ b. 1,000 miles away.
   - □ c. 135 miles away.

3. What is magma?
   - □ a. the name of a volcano
   - □ b. melted rock
   - □ c. the earth's outer shell

4. Mount Saint Helens had been inactive from
   - □ a. 1857 to 1980.
   - □ b. 1980 to 1987.
   - □ c. 1700 to 1900.

5. The eruption of this volcano
   - □ a. did not destroy any plants.
   - □ b. destroyed animal and plant life.
   - □ c. destroyed only animals.

Understanding the Passage

6. The Ring of Fire is located around the
   - □ a. Pacific Ocean.
   - □ b. Atlantic Ocean.
   - □ c. Indian Ocean.

7. Why does the area around Mount Saint Helens lack wildlife?
   - □ a. The soil is no longer fertile.
   - □ b. Hot gases are still present in the air.
   - □ c. The food chain has been partially destroyed.

8. What causes the eruption of a volcano?
   - □ a. plate friction within the earth
   - □ b. earthquakes around the volcano
   - □ c. a forest fire on the slopes of the volcano

9. Three materials of a volcano eruption are
   - □ a. hot gases, ashes, and magma.
   - □ b. air, fire, and ice.
   - □ c. rocks, sand, and fire.

10. Most volcanic activity occurs around the
    - □ a. Arctic Ocean.
    - □ b. Pacific Ocean.
    - □ c. Atlantic Ocean.

Busy Little Carpenters

Most people think of termites when they think of insects that live in wood. But there are other kinds of wood-nesting insects. Unlike termites, carpenter ants and carpenter bees do not eat wood. They must chew tunnels in wood to make their nests, though. They can do just as much damage as termites in this way.

Carpenter ants are easy to spot. They are large and reddish-brown or black. Workers are from ¼ to ½ inch long. The workers have strong jaws and will bite when disturbed. Indoors, the ants feed on sweets and other foods.

A colony of carpenter ants is started by a mated queen. The queen seeks damp wood for her nest. Once started, the nest is moved into dry, sound wood. The ants carve out their living quarters. They keep them clean and smooth. Sawdust from the nest is carried outside and dumped. If you see large ants around the house, beware! It is usually the first sign of a nest. The nest may not be inside, however. It may be in a stump or hollow tree near the house. But who knows when they might decide to move in.

Wood that has become damp should be watched carefully. Places that come under attack are porch pillars and supporting timbers. Other places to look are sills, joists, studs, and window and door trim. It is a good idea to poke the dampened wood with a sharp object. If the wood gives way and ants come tumbling out, the nest has likely been found.

Besides carpenter ants, there are carpenter bees. Carpenter bees look a lot like bumblebees. They range in size from ¼ to an inch long. Some are as large as bumblebees. However, carpenter bees have bare, shiny abdomens. The abdomens of bumblebees are covered with rows of thick yellow hair.

Carpenter bees cut an entrance hole across the grain of the wood. Then, they build their homes with the grain of the wood. They usually build their nests in dead twigs or branches. The damage caused by one or two bees is slight. But if they are not stopped, they can cause much damage over a long period.

By watching the bees, the nests can usually be found. It's a good idea to stop them before they spread and cause problems. The only good way to control pests is to poison their nests.

Recalling Facts

1. What color are carpenter ants?
   - ☐ a. dark gray and white
   - ☐ b. reddish-brown or black
   - ☐ c. white and yellow

2. How big are carpenter ant workers?
   - ☐ a. ¼ to ½ inch long
   - ☐ b. ½ to ¾ inch long
   - ☐ c. ¾ to 1 inch long

3. The queen carpenter ant first makes her nest in
   - ☐ a. cement walls.
   - ☐ b. damp wood.
   - ☐ c. old newspapers.

4. Carpenter bees look a lot like
   - ☐ a. bumblebees.
   - ☐ b. hornets.
   - ☐ c. termites.

5. Carpenter bees have bare, shiny
   - ☐ a. abdomens.
   - ☐ b. heads.
   - ☐ c. legs.

Understanding the Passage

6. Termites eat
   - ☐ a. bees.
   - ☐ b. grass.
   - ☐ c. wood.

7. Carpenter ants and carpenter bees destroy wood by
   - ☐ a. eating it.
   - ☐ b. nesting in it.
   - ☐ c. wetting it.

8. The head of the carpenter ant colony is the
   - ☐ a. soldier.
   - ☐ b. queen.
   - ☐ c. worker.

9. We can see that carpenter ants keep their nests
   - ☐ a. dirty and untidy.
   - ☐ b. neat and clean.
   - ☐ c. slimy and wet.

10. This article hints that carpenter ants and carpenter bees
    - ☐ a. are helpful to man.
    - ☐ b. fight each other.
    - ☐ c. live in groups.

18　Order in the Court

A court is a place where people go to settle their differences. There are two kinds of courts in America. One type is set up by the federal government. The second type is set up by the state.

The Supreme Court is the highest court in our country. It meets in Washington, D.C., in the Supreme Court Building. There are nine justices who sit on the court. They are appointed by the President and confirmed by the Senate. Once appointed, the justices serve for life.

One justice is picked to head the court. He is called the Chief Justice. The other eight are called Associate Justices.

When a case comes to the Supreme Court, the justices hear it together. The decision of more than half of the justices decides a case. When a decision is made, it is final. All other courts of our land must follow the decisions of the Supreme Court.

A Supreme Court is needed because the U.S. Congress or a state may pass a law that takes away a right of the people or a right of a state. A case involving such a law can be taken to the Supreme Court. The Supreme Court may decide that the law is unconstitutional. This means that the law does not have to be obeyed.

There are other courts lower than the Supreme Court. These are called Federal Courts. Most cases that reach Federal Courts are first heard in district courts. These are the lowest type of Federal Courts. If a person does not agree with the decision of the district court, he or she can take the case to a higher court. When this is done, he or she is appealing the case. The next highest court is the court of appeals. It ranks above the district court. Some kinds of cases can be taken from a court of appeals to the Supreme Court. At times, however, a case may go directly to the Supreme Court. It may skip the appeals court altogether.

Each state has a system of courts, too. These courts help to explain the laws of that state. These courts also hear the trials of persons who are accused of having broken state laws. They also hear cases about personal rights and property rights. The states have both higher and lower courts.

It is everyone's duty to obey the law as explained by the courts.

*Reading Time*_____　*Comprehension Score*_____　*Words per Minute*_____　**49**

Recalling Facts

1. The highest court in our country is the
   - ☐ a. Appeals Court.
   - ☐ b. District Court.
   - ☐ c. Supreme Court.

2. The Supreme Court is located in
   - ☐ a. Chicago.
   - ☐ b. New York.
   - ☐ c. Washington, D.C.

3. Most cases that reach Federal Courts are first heard in
   - ☐ a. district courts.
   - ☐ b. small claims court.
   - ☐ c. supreme courts.

4. Each state has a system of courts to help explain the
   - ☐ a. Bill of Rights.
   - ☐ b. Constitution.
   - ☐ c. laws.

5. State courts hear cases about personal rights and
   - ☐ a. property rights.
   - ☐ b. religious rights.
   - ☐ c. federal rights.

Understanding the Passage

6. What is this article mostly about?
   - ☐ a. court justices and the U.S. Senate
   - ☐ b. small claims courts of America
   - ☐ c. the Supreme Court and Federal Courts

7. The President picks nine justices to sit on the
   - ☐ a. Appeals Court.
   - ☐ b. Superior Court.
   - ☐ c. Supreme Court.

8. Associate Justices are under the
   - ☐ a. Chief Justice.
   - ☐ b. Head Justice.
   - ☐ c. General Justice.

9. The Supreme Court would probably make decisions on
   - ☐ a. car accidents.
   - ☐ b. robberies.
   - ☐ c. states' rights.

10. When you appeal a case, you
    - ☐ a. forget about it completely.
    - ☐ b. take it to a higher court.
    - ☐ c. talk about it with a lawyer.

19 Garden Flowers

Farmers and gardeners in North America raise about 30,000 species of flowers. Many kinds of flowering plants are grown for food. But most are garden flowers, grown for decoration.

Most garden flowers are herbaceous plants. These are plants that do not have woody stems. But others, like golden bells and spiraea, are woody stemmed. Many garden flowers need bright sunlight. Others grow better in the shade. Some need large amounts of water. Others grow best in well-drained soil.

Most garden flowers also grow wild, or had ancestors that grew wild. Some are exactly the same as the wild kind. Gardeners have bred others to produce hardier stems, larger or different colored flowers, or more attractive leaves. Often these changes are temporary. The plants may change back to their wild form within a few generations. The gardener must continue to care only for the best plants and destroy the others. This makes for a better selection of flowers.

Flowers are grouped by their life span. Annuals live only one year. But this term is also used for any plants that bloom within a year after seeds are planted. Most annuals are easy to grow. But gardeners must plant many seeds because some may not sprout. If too many seeds sprout, then the weakest plants are weeded out.

Most annuals bloom two to three months after the seeds are planted. When they begin to bloom, the blossoms are removed before they seed. This allows the plants to produce more flowers over a longer period. Common annuals are cornflowers, zinnias, marigolds, and sweet peas.

Biennials live for two years after the seeds are planted. Most biennials bloom well only during the second year. Gardeners usually plant them in midsummer. The flowers then bloom the next spring. Biennials are often used in formal flower beds while others make fine borders or backgrounds. Common examples are hollyhocks, snapdragons, foxgloves, and Canterbury bells.

The seeds of perennials are usually planted in early spring or in midsummer. The flowers bloom the following year. Roses and other flowers with woody stems may live for a long time. Gardeners usually plant perennial seeds in an area where they are protected from weather. In fall, they move the seedlings to a place with proper soil and sunlight. Most perennials spread by sending out shoots from their roots. Common perennials are asters, daisies, irises, and violets.

*Reading Time*_____ *Comprehension Score*_____ *Words per Minute*_____

Recalling Facts

1. Annual flowers live
   □ a. one year.
   □ b. two years.
   □ c. for a long time.

2. Biennial flowers live
   □ a. one year.
   □ b. two years.
   □ c. for a long time.

3. Perennial flowers live
   □ a. one year.
   □ b. two years.
   □ c. for a long time.

4. A common type of flowering annual is a
   □ a. rose.
   □ b. violet.
   □ c. cornflower.

5. Flowers are classified by their
   □ a. life span.
   □ b. fragrance.
   □ c. color.

Understanding the Passage

6. What would be an appropriate title for this selection?
   □ a. How to Fight Garden Pests
   □ b. Garden Design and Color
   □ c. Annuals, Biennials, and Perennials

7. Flowering plants are not grown for
   □ a. food.
   □ b. decoration.
   □ c. medicine.

8. Gardeners breed wildflowers to produce
   □ a. hardier stems.
   □ b. larger roots.
   □ c. smaller flowers.

9. What must all flowering plants have to grow?
   □ a. bright sunlight
   □ b. dark shade
   □ c. water

10. Perennial seedlings are moved in the
   □ a. spring.
   □ b. fall.
   □ c. summer.

Reaching the top of a mountain is a thrilling experience. But like many exciting sports, mountain climbing can be dangerous. The urge to conquer high places makes many people take chances and forget safety rules.

Good climbers take precautions. None of the explorers of Mount Everest would have made it home if they had not planned ahead. So if you have never hiked before, take the time to learn some simple safety tips.

First, don't try to climb a mountain alone. Plan ahead of time. Let someone know where you are going and when they should expect you back.

Know ahead of time where the nearest ranger station is. Stay on the marked roads and trails. Look for landmarks as you move through the woods.

It is important that you be properly equipped. You should have maps, a compass, a flashlight, matches, a knife, a first aid kit, and warm clothes. Bring plenty of high-energy food like raisins and peanuts. Make sure you have water with you.

If you do get lost, don't panic. Sit down a few minutes and catch your breath. Then look around to see where you are. You could climb a tree for a better view. Look for familiar landmarks. If the country is hilly, going downhill is best. You are more likely to find streams and rivers that way, and these lead to houses and towns. You can also look for telephone poles and follow the wires. Even in the middle of the Grand Canyon, there are telephone poles!

Rest when you need to; don't get overtired. Avoid dangerous cliffs or steep slides. Be sure to stay warm and dry. At night, you can light a signal fire. This will keep you warm, and maybe you can cook on it too. But keep water handy and don't let the fire get out of control.

If you get hungry, be careful not to eat things unless you know what they are. One idea is to kill a porcupine. This sounds strange, but it is easy to do with a rock. Porcupines move very slowly and are protected from hunters by law so that people who are lost in the woods can eat them.

Above all, remain calm. Know what you are doing before you leave, and be prepared for emergencies. The biggest thrill of mountain climbing is reaching your goal by being in control.

Recalling Facts

1. When mountain climbing, make sure you
   - ☐ a. always hike alone.
   - ☐ b. bring along a good book.
   - ☐ c. know where the nearest ranger station is.

2. When you go mountain climbing, you should
   - ☐ a. let someone know where you've gone.
   - ☐ b. go alone.
   - ☐ c. take provisions for a long hike.

3. If you get lost, you could
   - ☐ a. climb a tree.
   - ☐ b. whistle loudly.
   - ☐ c. plan to stay the night.

4. When you go mountain climbing, you should carry a
   - ☐ a. map.
   - ☐ b. tent.
   - ☐ c. weapon.

5. When you walk through the woods, you should look for
   - ☐ a. caves.
   - ☐ b. landmarks.
   - ☐ c. wildlife.

Understanding the Passage

6. This article hints that mountain climbing can be dangerous if you are not
   - ☐ a. educated.
   - ☐ b. healthy.
   - ☐ c. prepared.

7. It's a good idea to mountain climb with a
   - ☐ a. child.
   - ☐ b. friend.
   - ☐ c. pet.

8. When you go hiking, you should travel on
   - ☐ a. hilly cliffs.
   - ☐ b. marked trails.
   - ☐ c. steep slides.

9. If you get lost in the woods, you should
   - ☐ a. lie flat.
   - ☐ b. stay calm.
   - ☐ c. yell and scream.

10. The article suggests that a signal fire
    - ☐ a. has more than one use.
    - ☐ b. tends to flare out of control.
    - ☐ c. may be difficult to light.

You have found a home you want to buy. What is the next step? Very likely you will need a mortgage loan to pay for your home. Most families do pay a good part of the purchase price of a home with a mortgage.

A mortgage is a loan contract. A bank agrees to provide the money you need to buy a certain home. You, in turn, agree to repay the money based on terms stated in the agreement.

The size of each payment depends on three things. The first is the amount of money you have borrowed. The second thing is the interest rate charged by the bank. The third thing is the number of years you need to pay the loan off. Under law, the contract has to state the amount of the loan, the interest you will pay, and the size and times of the payments. Any other charges made by the bank must also be included in the contract.

As the borrower, you must promise your home as security for the loan. It remains pledged until the loan is paid off. If you fail to meet the terms of the contract, the bank has the right to foreclose. Under the law, this means that the bank can take your home and sell it to pay off the loan.

Most mortgages are installment loans. This means that you are required to make a fixed payment—usually once a month. Part of the payment is kept by the bank to cover the interest charges. Part of it may be set aside by the bank to pay your taxes and insurance. And part of the payment reduces the principal of the loan. The principal is the actual amount that you borrowed.

In the beginning, most of each payment goes for the interest. As you keep paying, a smaller share of each payment is for interest and a larger share repays the principal. As your payments reduce the amount you owe on the principal of the loan, the interest charges are reduced.

You build up equity in your home as you pay off the mortgage. Equity is that part of your home which you own free from the bank. When the last payment on the mortgage is made, you will have full equity. The home will be completely yours. The interest has been paid off. The principal has been repaid in full.

Recalling Facts

1. In order to pay for a new home, usually you must apply for
   ☐ a. an account.
   ☐ b. a job.
   ☐ c. a loan.

2. A mortgage is a
   ☐ a. checking account.
   ☐ b. loan contract.
   ☐ c. tax return.

3. Which of the following is not included in a mortgage payment?
   ☐ a. interest
   ☐ b. equity
   ☐ c. principal

4. The actual amount borrowed is called the
   ☐ a. contract.
   ☐ b. principal.
   ☐ c. repayment.

5. That part of your home that you own free from the bank is called
   ☐ a. equity.
   ☐ b. insurance.
   ☐ c. security.

Understanding the Passage

6. This article hints that
   ☐ a. banks will not lend money to families.
   ☐ b. many people borrow money to buy a house.
   ☐ c. older homes are not worth buying.

7. We can guess from this article that
   ☐ a. banks don't like to give mortgages.
   ☐ b. mortgage payments vary greatly.
   ☐ c. new houses don't need insurance.

8. If you do not meet your monthly payments, the bank has the right to
   ☐ a. decorate your home.
   ☐ b. destroy your home.
   ☐ c. sell your home.

9. During the first few years of paying a mortgage, most of your monthly payment goes for
   ☐ a. interest.
   ☐ b. taxes.
   ☐ c. insurance.

10. When is your equity in your home the greatest?
    ☐ a. before you begin your payments
    ☐ b. during the first few years of your payments
    ☐ c. toward the end of your payments

Most manuscripts can be traced to a certain period of history by their materials. In ancient times, papyrus, wood, and wax tablets, parchment, or vellum were used. During the Middle Ages, parchment and paper were used. And in modern times, paper is used for books.

Papyrus was first written on in Egypt about 4,500 years ago. The Egyptians prepared the writing material from the reedlike plant. It was cut in strips and pressed. The manuscript sheets were pasted together into rolls. These "volumes" were 20 to 30 feet long. Many were even longer. The British Museum has copies of the Egyptian *Book of the Dead* which are ● 100 feet long.

There are papyrus manuscripts that date from 2500 B.C. Others were written on as late as 1000 A.D. Papyrus was used in all lands around the Mediterranean. Scholars believe that all great Greek and Roman works were written on papyrus.

Wax tablets usually had a wooden frame. They look like the 19th century slates used in American schools. In ancient times, these tablets were used in many ways. School exercises, letters, and contracts were written on them. They were also used to write other more formal documents. Sometimes two or three tablets were tied together. ●

The use of skins for writing material is as old as the invention of writing. But parchment books did not become popular in Europe until 1300 A.D. They were very scarce and only for the rich. Parchment is also called vellum. It was first used because of its durability. It is also easier to write on with a pen. Scribes of the Middle Ages copied many ancient works on parchment from decaying papyrus. The Greek poetry of Sappho was copied in this way.

Palimpsest is a type of parchment that could be reused. It was washed ● and old documents recopied on it. Hundreds of palimpsests exist, but they are often in small pieces. The first text can still be read on some examples. Cicero's *Republic* was handed down from a palimpsest.

The Chinese knew how to make paper by 1000 A.D. But the western world did not learn the secret until the Crusades. During the 1400s, paper took the place of parchment. However, parchment was still used for legal reasons for some years. Most valuable paper manuscripts of the West belong to modern times. A collection of valuable American manuscripts is in the United States National Archives in Washington, D.C.

Recalling Facts

1. Modern manuscripts are written on
   □ a. parchment.
   □ b. paper.
   □ c. papyrus.

2. Vellum is another word for
   □ a. paper.
   □ b. parchment.
   □ c. a wax tablet.

3. Most Greek and Roman books were written on
   □ a. parchment.
   □ b. vellum.
   □ c. papyrus.

4. How long is the Egyptian *Book of the Dead*?
   □ a. ten feet
   □ b. twenty feet
   □ c. one hundred feet

5. Paper was invented by the
   □ a. Egyptians.
   □ b. Americans.
   □ c. Chinese.

Understanding the Passage

6. What is the main idea of this selection?
   □ a. Manuscripts have been made of different materials.
   □ b. Most modern westerners read books.
   □ c. Many modern Chinese read books.

7. What is the oldest form of writing material?
   □ a. skins
   □ b. paper
   □ c. papyrus

8. A palimpsest is
   □ a. an ancient form of writing.
   □ b. a type of parchment.
   □ c. decaying papyrus.

9. Parchment was used as a writing material because of its
   □ a. low cost.
   □ b. durability.
   □ c. many colors.

10. The western world did not know of paper until the
    □ a. 19th century.
    □ b. seventeenth century.
    □ c. fifteenth century.

23 Exotic Currencies

Some of the forms of currency that were used before coins were invented are still used in the world. Cowrie shells are one of the oldest forms of money. They are still used in the South Seas and in parts of Africa. Pearls and tooth, clam, and bailer shells are used in the South Seas. Strings of shell beads and even the backbones of sharks are also used. The native Americans used strings of wampum made from clam shells for money and decoration. There was white and purple or black wampum. The first white settlers to America used this to trade with the Indians.

On the west coast of North America, native Americans made shield-shaped plaques of various sizes. They were of copper, painted and engraved with designs. One "copper" could be worth as much as 7,000 small, cotton blankets. (Blankets were a common form of money among these people.) Seal tusks, bone, and bronze fish hooks were also used for money by the Aleuts and North Pacific tribes.

In Mexico, the Aztecs produced money of metal. From gold, they made flat, human-shaped images which were used as a means of exchange. A strange blade-shaped piece of copper was also used as currency.

Africa has had many types of money because of its size and large number of tribes. Cowrie shells, ivory, coral, metal wire, and ostrich egg shells are among the various materials used. A British firm still makes bronze rings to ship to the west African coast. They have been in great demand there for a century as currency. Curious, flat copper crosses of a Belgian Congo tribe are used when a young man wants to take a wife. Also from the Congo come the spear "coins." These iron or copper spearheads are often a foot long.

One of the strangest forms of money is the stone currency of the Yap Island in the Pacific. They are made of flat slabs of limestone. The smaller ones are sometimes about ten inches across, while the larger are ten feet across. All have a center hole where a pole is placed for carrying. The Yap people made voyages by canoe to the Palaus Islands, 300 miles away. Or they traveled to Guam to carve these stones from local quarries. Today, these large stones are not used for money. They are used for ceremonial purposes.

Recalling Facts

1. Metal was used as an early form of money in
   - □ a. Mexico.
   - □ b. the South Seas.
   - □ c. the Caribbean Islands.

2. One copper plaque of the Pacific Coast tribes
   - □ a. was sewn to a blanket.
   - □ b. could be worth 7,000 blankets.
   - □ c. could be worth 7,000 seal tusks.

3. The most curious form of early currency was the
   - □ a. American dollar bill.
   - □ b. Spanish peseta.
   - □ c. stone slab of Yap Island.

4. Which geographical area seems to have the most forms of money?
   - □ a. Africa
   - □ b. North America
   - □ c. South America

5. Which type of money is used in marriage?
   - □ a. copper crosses of the Belgian Congo
   - □ b. wampum beads of native Americans
   - □ c. stone slabs of the Yap Islanders

Understanding the Passage

6. Another title for this selection could be
   - □ a. Trade Throughout the World.
   - □ b. A Standard Form of Currency.
   - □ c. The Different Materials of Money.

7. This selection hints that
   - □ a. money has not been important to many societies.
   - □ b. money has been important to many societies.
   - □ c. metal money is used everywhere.

8. Pearls are used as
   - □ a. money in the South Seas.
   - □ b. decoration in Yap Island.
   - □ c. jewelry in the Belgian Congo.

9. The stone currency of Yap Island is
   - □ a. still used as a form of money.
   - □ b. of the same size.
   - □ c. carved in Guam or the Palaus Islands.

10. We can see from this selection that the Aleuts
    - □ a. used three types of currency.
    - □ b. did not use any type of currency.
    - □ c. used whale bone as a type of currency.

24 Think Thin

Persons who are overweight should watch their diet carefully in order to lose pounds. The best way to do this is to start a weight control program. At first it is wise to talk with your doctor. He can tell you if your health is good enough for you to try to lose weight. If you are in good health, your doctor can tell you how much weight you should lose. He can advise you of the number of calories you should have in your meals each day. He can tell you about exercising while on your diet. A good rule is to lose slowly. ●
A loss of a pound or two a week is plenty.

Plan meals around foods you know. The best diet for you is the one you can be faithful to. This means that it is wise to include foods that you are used to and that are part of your regular eating habits. Strange foods may not satisfy you. They may throw you off your diet. When you have lost the weight you wish, simple items can be added to your diet so that you can maintain the weight you want. While you are dieting, try to build a pattern ●
of eating that you can follow later to maintain your desired weight. Strange and glamorous foods used on a diet may work but will be hard to continue eating afterwards. As a result, you may become discouraged and go back to the old habits that put on the extra weight in the first place.

When you plan meals, follow a sound food plan. Be sure to include the daily nutrition you need. Make certain you are getting the right kinds of food.

When dieting, choose low-calorie foods. Avoid such items as fats, gravy, sauce, fried food, sweets, cakes, alcoholic drinks or soft drinks, and cream. ●
Use spices, herbs, or tart fruit juices to season your food.

Learn to like cereal or fruit with little or no sugar added. Try to take coffee and tea without sugar or cream. Snacks can be part of your diet. For example, a piece of fruit or a crisp vegetable, or a simple dessert saved from mealtime, can be eaten between meals.

Keep busy! This way you will not be tempted to go off the diet. Take advantage of opportunities to exercise. Try walking instead of riding whenever possible. Happy dieting!

Recalling Facts

1. The first thing to do if you want to lose weight is
   - ☐ a. stop eating breakfast.
   - ☐ b. talk to your doctor.
   - ☐ c. weigh yourself daily.

2. What is the most you should lose a week?
   - ☐ a. one or two pounds
   - ☐ b. five or six pounds
   - ☐ c. ten or twelve pounds

3. When dieting, you should choose
   - ☐ a. high-protein foods.
   - ☐ b. high-starch foods.
   - ☐ c. low-calorie foods.

4. Which of the following should be included in a good diet?
   - ☐ a. alcoholic drinks
   - ☐ b. crisp vegetables
   - ☐ c. fried foods

5. A good diet snack would be a
   - ☐ a. candy bar.
   - ☐ b. piece of fruit.
   - ☐ c. sweet cake.

Understanding the Passage

6. This article tells us
   - ☐ a. about fad diets.
   - ☐ b. how to diet.
   - ☐ c. why we should diet.

7. Which of the following would *not* be a good diet food?
   - ☐ a. carrots
   - ☐ b. french fries
   - ☐ c. steak

8. This article suggests that when you diet you should also
   - ☐ a. exercise.
   - ☐ b. fast.
   - ☐ c. relax.

9. What can we conclude from this article?
   - ☐ a. Doctors do not like to put people on diets.
   - ☐ b. Only people who are in good health should diet.
   - ☐ c. Weight control is not necessary for overweight people.

10. Tart fruit juices can be used to
   - ☐ a. clean foods.
   - ☐ b. flavor foods.
   - ☐ c. preserve foods.

Backpacking offers freedom found in no other type of wilderness travel. However, you must know what to expect when you hike off into the wilderness. There will be no table to eat from and no grill to hold your pots and pans. There will be few trail signs to guide you. You must know how to follow a map. You will be on your own.

Still, there are countless places you can go. Try an overnight trip to a mountain or stream. Follow an unmarked trail that seems inviting. A trial run will help to tone up muscles and show up mistakes in plans. During a short trip, you will not suffer too badly if something has been left at home.

Experienced backpackers pride themselves on being able to travel light. With many, weight saving is a game. Some cut towels in half and saw the handles off toothbrushes to save ounces. They measure out just the right amount of food needed and put it in plastic bags. Plastic bags are lighter than cardboard. There are dozens of tricks to save ounces that add up to pounds.

Footwear is an important thing to keep in mind. Sneakers are cool and cheap. For youngsters who are growing, the heavy-soled, ankle-high sneaker is best. Rubber is good where the going is wet. Hikers in swamps and bogs prefer the shoepac above anything else. However, leather is the most popular shoe material for all-around hiking. It wears well and is soft. It can be waterproofed to shed snow and rain.

Leather soles on boots are slippery. Most hikers use rubber or cord soles. When the soles wear out, thick rubber lug soles can be put on. These grip the rocks well.

Hiking boots should fit comfortably over two pairs of socks, one thin and one thick. They should protect the ankles and support the foot. They must be able to withstand long mileage on rocks and roots. Be sure that boots are well broken in before the trip. A mountain trail is no place to break in a new pair of boots. Make sure also to use the proper type of footwear for hiking. Ski boots are for skiing and cowboy boots are for horseback riding. Footwear with eyelets and lacing have proved best for hiking. A wise hiker always brings an extra pair of laces.

Recalling Facts

1. When backpacking, you must
   know how to follow a
   - ☐ a. graph.
   - ☐ b. manual.
   - ☐ c. map.

2. A trial run at backpacking
   helps to tone up your
   - ☐ a. bones.
   - ☐ b. muscles.
   - ☐ c. speech.

3. In order to travel light,
   some backpackers cut the
   handles off
   - ☐ a. grills.
   - ☐ b. pots.
   - ☐ c. toothbrushes.

4. Rubber soles are good when
   the going is
   - ☐ a. rocky.
   - ☐ b. smooth.
   - ☐ c. wet.

5. What is the most popular shoe
   material for all-around hiking?
   - ☐ a. plastic
   - ☐ b. rubber
   - ☐ c. leather

Understanding the Passage

6. Backpacking is similar to
   - ☐ a. hiking.
   - ☐ b. skiing.
   - ☐ c. swimming.

7. Backpackers
   - ☐ a. cannot read simple maps.
   - ☐ b. do not carry heavy items.
   - ☐ c. wear leather cowboy boots.

8. Cardboard is heavier than
   - ☐ a. pots and pans.
   - ☐ b. plastic bags.
   - ☐ c. tin cans.

9. Leather boots can be
   - ☐ a. shrunk.
   - ☐ b. stretched.
   - ☐ c. waterproofed.

10. Rubber lug soles are good for
    - ☐ a. flooded areas.
    - ☐ b. freezing temperatures.
    - ☐ c. rocky surfaces.

A Stroke of Lightning

Lightning is a giant flash of light in the sky caused by an electrical charge. The current can flow between parts of one cloud. This is called intracloud lightning. A current flowing between different clouds is called cloud-to-cloud lightning. The current can also flow between clouds and the earth.

Lightning between clouds does not cause any damage on earth. The electrical energy is dispersed into the air. But lightning between a cloud and earth can kill a person, start a forest fire, or destroy property.

When a thundercloud becomes charged, the whole cloud is charged. The cloud has many small water droplets. Each droplet has a surface charge. Thus, a cloud may have great electric potential. When a charged cloud is near the earth's surface, the ground develops an opposite charge. If a cloud comes near an opposite electric charge, a huge spark occurs.

The air that separates the cloud and earth is an insulator. It resists efforts of the opposite charges of electricity to rush together. But when the electrical current is large enough, it overcomes air resistance. Then, a lightning flash happens.

A flash between a cloud and earth may measure eight miles long. It may travel one million feet per second. One stroke of lightning can measure more than fifteen million volts. Lightning that goes between oppositely-charged clouds can be twenty miles long.

As lightning travels, it heats the air in its path. This sudden heating causes the air to expand. The cool air farther away is pressed into a smaller space. This starts a great air wave that ends in thunder.

All strokes of lightning are the same. But they have different forms that depend on the position of the observer. Chain or zigzag lightning is a chain of bright light which zigzags. It actually follows a winding path like a river. A single stroke of this lightning often breaks into forks or branches.

Sheet lightning has no specific form. It's usually a bright flash that lights the sky. Sheet lightning is really light from a flash of chain lightning beyond the horizon.

Heat lightning is often seen on summer evenings. It's the same as sheet lightning, but the flashes are fainter. This lightning happens too far away for thunder to be heard.

Ball lightning differs from these other forms. It appears as a glowing ball that floats several seconds before disappearing. It never reaches earth.

Recalling Facts

1. What is lightning?
   - ☐ a. a flash of light
   - ☐ b. a great air wave
   - ☐ c. an insulator

2. The air that separates the earth and clouds is
   - ☐ a. an electrical current.
   - ☐ b. an insulator.
   - ☐ c. a lightning flash.

3. What part of a thundercloud becomes charged?
   - ☐ a. the top part
   - ☐ b. the entire cloud
   - ☐ c. the bottom part

4. How long can intracloud lightning be?
   - ☐ a. thirty miles long
   - ☐ b. twenty miles long
   - ☐ c. ten miles long

5. Which type of lightning has no specific form?
   - ☐ a. sheet lightning
   - ☐ b. ball lightning
   - ☐ c. chain lightning

Understanding the Passage

6. A good title for this selection could be
   - ☐ a. Different Forms of Lightning.
   - ☐ b. The Uses of Electricity.
   - ☐ c. Safety in a Thunderstorm.

7. It seems that some lightning can
   - ☐ a. kill a person.
   - ☐ b. provide electricity for human use.
   - ☐ c. put out a forest fire.

8. Thunder may not accompany
   - ☐ a. ball lightning.
   - ☐ b. heat lightning.
   - ☐ c. chain lightning.

9. Another name for chain lightning is
   - ☐ a. heat lightning.
   - ☐ b. sheet lightning.
   - ☐ c. zigzag lightning.

10. Lightning can travel
   - ☐ a. 100,000 feet per second.
   - ☐ b. 1,000 feet per second.
   - ☐ c. 1,000,000 feet per second.

27 Keep Looking Up

Bird-watching can be fun. One of the first things for the beginning bird-watcher to learn is how to recognize common birds by their shapes. Many parts of a bird's body give clues to its identity. Things to look at are body shape and size. Look at the length and shape of the tail, too. The wing shape, bill type, and leg length are still other clues. Where a bird makes its nest helps to tell us what it is.

First, consider the tail. Some tails are forked, like a barn swallow's. Some tails are round, like a blue jay's, or pointed, like a dove's. A mockingbird has a long tail, while the robin's tail is medium length. Some birds, like the woodpecker, use their tails as a brace against the tree trunk.

A look at a bird's beak can help to identify it. Hawks and owls have the large, hooked beaks of meat eaters. The vulture has a less sharply hooked beak. Woodpeckers need long, strong beaks for tapping away at trees all day. The kingfisher's long, pointed beak helps it catch fish more easily. The nighthawk has a very small beak for its size. Its mouth opens wide, however, to scoop in insects while it flies.

Beaks can also help you tell the difference between birds of similar shapes. For instance, the blue jay and the cardinal are shaped alike. When it is dark and you cannot see the color, you can confuse the two birds because of their shapes. The cardinal, however, has a short, thick bill. It is a seed eater. The blue jay is the one with the long and thin beak.

Many birds look alike when they fly. It can be hard to tell them apart by their shapes when they are high in the sky. Geese and cranes may both fly in V-shaped flocks, but other things are different. Cranes fly with their long necks and legs outstretched. Geese also fly with long necks outstretched, but their shorter legs do not go beyond their tail feathers. Herons, although they look like cranes, fly with their long necks folded in an "S" shape.

Keep these hints in mind when you bird-watch. See which birds you can recognize. Be aware that it takes time to learn all of the things that an expert bird-watcher must know. No one can become an expert bird-watcher overnight.

Recalling Facts

1. The beginner bird-watcher should learn how to recognize birds by their
   - ☐ a. colors.
   - ☐ b. feathers.
   - ☐ c. shapes.

2. The barn swallow's tail is
   - ☐ a. forked.
   - ☐ b. pointed.
   - ☐ c. round.

3. Hawks and owls have large hooked
   - ☐ a. beaks.
   - ☐ b. claws.
   - ☐ c. tails.

4. The nighthawk feeds while it
   - ☐ a. flies.
   - ☐ b. mates.
   - ☐ c. sleeps.

5. Herons look like
   - ☐ a. blue jays.
   - ☐ b. cranes.
   - ☐ c. woodpeckers.

Understanding the Passage

6. Choose the best title for this article.
   - ☐ a. Know Your Birds
   - ☐ b. The Life of the Blue Jay
   - ☐ c. Woodpeckers as Pets

7. You can identify birds by looking at their
   - ☐ a. bodies.
   - ☐ b. enemies.
   - ☐ c. food.

8. Meat-eating birds have
   - ☐ a. big, hooked beaks.
   - ☐ b. long, strong beaks.
   - ☐ c. short, rounded beaks.

9. We can guess that the kingfisher lives near
   - ☐ a. deserts.
   - ☐ b. lakes.
   - ☐ c. mountains.

10. If a bird has a short, thick bill, it probably eats
   - ☐ a. insects.
   - ☐ b. meat.
   - ☐ c. seeds.

A mixer in the kitchen can speed up your work. It can make your work easier. This wonderful invention can stir sauces and gravies. A mixer can mash potatoes. It can cream sugar and shortening. And, of course, a mixer can mix batters. Mixers come in three styles: portable, stand, and convertible.

The portable mixer is held in your hand. You direct the pair of beaters around a pan or bowl. This type of mixer has a light-duty electric motor. It uses from 100 to 150 watts of current. It is mainly used to stir thin batters. Models with higher wattage can stir thicker mixtures. A portable mixer can be used to make packaged cakes, puddings, and gelatin. It is useful for whipping cream and beating eggs. And, it is easy to store. It can be kept in a drawer or hung on a wall.

Unlike the portable mixer, the stand mixer has a rather heavy frame with the mixer head at the top. There is a wide base big enough for large bowls or a bowl turntable. To make sure that things get mixed properly, the beaters usually turn the bowl and turntable as they mix. Some stand mixers use from 200 to 400 watts of electricity. Those with high ratings can mix thick batters and mix bread dough. Because of their size and weight, stand mixers are usually left in place on a kitchen counter.

The convertible mixer is similar to the stand type mixer except that the head can be removed for portable use or storage. Heads of heavy-duty models, however, may be tiring to hold.

On all mixers, speed control switches or dials should be well located. They should be easy to read. They should have an "off" setting for safety. Some mixer controls only have settings for high, medium, or low speeds. Other mixers have speed controls that have a better range.

Some mixers have extra attachments or parts you can buy. For instance, bowl sets, plastic beaters for non-stick pans, and hooks for mixing dough are all extras. You can get wire whisk beaters for whipping and flat beaters for creaming. Some of these things may be added at no extra cost when you buy your mixer. Other attachments may have to be bought separately.

Almost all attachments have one thing in common—they make kitchen work a little easier.

Recalling Facts

1. A mixer can cream sugar and
   - ☐ a. eggs.
   - ☐ b. flour.
   - ☐ c. shortening.

2. How many types of mixers are there?
   - ☐ a. three
   - ☐ b. four
   - ☐ c. five

3. A portable mixer is mainly used to stir
   - ☐ a. bread dough.
   - ☐ b. thick batters.
   - ☐ c. thin batters.

4. The stand mixer has a heavy
   - ☐ a. cord.
   - ☐ b. frame.
   - ☐ c. handle.

5. How much electricity does a stand mixer use?
   - ☐ a. 50–100 watts
   - ☐ b. 100–150 watts
   - ☐ c. 200–400 watts

Understanding the Passage

6. Choose the best title for this article.
   - ☐ a. Different Kinds of Mixers
   - ☐ b. Electricity Makes the Difference
   - ☐ c. Tasty Desserts

7. The portable mixer is probably
   - ☐ a. dangerous.
   - ☐ b. lightweight.
   - ☐ c. pretty.

8. The stand mixer is not easy to
   - ☐ a. sell.
   - ☐ b. store.
   - ☐ c. use.

9. The convertible mixer and the stand mixer are
   - ☐ a. expensive.
   - ☐ b. rustproof.
   - ☐ c. similar.

10. Many mixers have
    - ☐ a. extra parts.
    - ☐ b. guide plates.
    - ☐ c. sharp edges.

Get Along, Little Cowboy

Men who take care of large herds of cattle are called cowboys. The American cowboy has always been a symbol of the "Wild West." Cowboys became famous for their sad songs. They were well known for their long tales about the cattle drives on western trails. Being a cowboy was hard, lonely work.

In the old days, cowboys were called cowpokes or cowpunchers. This was because of the sticks they used to poke the cows onto loading ramps. Many cowboys today like to be called cowhands. This is because they are hired hands.

A cowhand's clothing has not changed much from the early days. His pants must be tight. Loose or flapping trousers may catch brush as he chases the cows. His pants are still called "Levis." The broad-brimmed hat the cowhand wears was made to keep the sun and the wind out of his eyes. The hat's deep crown helps to keep the hat on his head when he is riding very fast. The deep-crowned hat can also be used as a bucket. From this we get the name ten-gallon hat.

The cowhand wears high-heeled boots for very practical reasons, also. The heel gives him a hold in the stirrup. The length of the boot supports his ankles and keeps him warm. The cowboy's neckerchief can be pulled over his face to protect him from the dust.

The cowboy's horse is very valuable to him. A sure-footed horse can mean the difference between life and death on the trail. Almost every cowhand today owns a horse of his own. Some cowhands have six different horses. A good horse and a strong rope have long been thought of as a cowhand's work tools. The rope is his most important tool. He uses it to catch cattle and to hold his horse. He may even use it to pull wagons across muddy rivers. Early ropes were made of horsehair, grass, or henequen. Most ropes today are made of nylon.

The life of a cowboy today has not changed much since the old days. On large ranches, he does have some machines. Even pickup trucks help him in his work. But he must still know how to ride well. He must be able to spend long hours in the saddle with little food and in all kinds of weather. And, of course, today's cowhands must know how to handle cattle.

Recalling Facts

1. The American cowboy became famous for his
   - ☐ a. good cooking.
   - ☐ b. rough manners.
   - ☐ c. sad songs.

2. Cowboys used to poke cattle with sticks to move them onto
   - ☐ a. flat beds.
   - ☐ b. grassy plains.
   - ☐ c. loading ramps.

3. Many cowboys today like to be called
   - ☐ a. cowhands.
   - ☐ b. cowpokes.
   - ☐ c. cowpunchers.

4. A cowboy's pants are called
   - ☐ a. breeches.
   - ☐ b. Lee's.
   - ☐ c. Levis.

5. Almost every cowhand today owns a
   - ☐ a. gun.
   - ☐ b. horse.
   - ☐ c. whip.

Understanding the Passage

6. In what part of America do you find cowboys?
   - ☐ a. North
   - ☐ b. South
   - ☐ c. West

7. Cowboys mostly work
   - ☐ a. in factories.
   - ☐ b. on trains.
   - ☐ c. outside.

8. Loose pants on a cowboy are
   - ☐ a. dangerous.
   - ☐ b. expensive.
   - ☐ c. stylish.

9. A ten-gallon hat is very
   - ☐ a. deep.
   - ☐ b. loose.
   - ☐ c. small.

10. Today's cowboy uses some modern
   - ☐ a. buildings.
   - ☐ b. equipment.
   - ☐ c. novels.

A baby spends the first year of life learning to listen. A newborn child comes equipped with a finely-tuned pair of ears, but he doesn't yet know how to use them. A buzz of meaningless noise surrounds him. No one sound means more than any other. Unlike his ears, the hearing center of his brain is still immature. As the baby grows, two things happen. First, he becomes better at picking out certain sounds. Second, he begins to remember them.

This development is easy to see. If you make a loud sound near a day-old baby's head, you will not see any reaction. Only a check on his pulse or breathing rate will show a change. But just two weeks later, the same noise will make him jerk. He may even turn his head toward you. Now the human voice means something to him. If he hears another baby crying, he may cry. By his fourth to sixth week, sounds like the doorbell or the closing of a door no longer surprise him. He can pick out one voice—his mother's—from all others. That one voice can soothe him and stop his crying. By eight weeks these mother-sounds can make him smile.

What is actually happening is that he is starting to learn to listen. He can select certain sounds and memorize them. When he hears that sound again, he can match it with the one he has heard before. These skills are basic to all learning.

At the same time these early hearing and language skills get under way, the child begins to practice making sounds. His first sounds are the *discomfort* sounds. These are the shrill whines that he seems to spend much of his time making. These sounds are heard when he is not quiet or sleeping. These sounds mean nothing to him yet. To his mother they say he is wet, uncomfortable, or hungry.

Within the baby's first month, another sound appears: the *comfort* sounds. These are different from the discomfort sounds. These are more throaty and vowel-like. These coos, sighs, and grunts are the beginnings of true speech. As the child grows, his comfort sounds will use more of the vowels and consonants and rhythms which he will later use. These sounds will come together to form the first word. This special event will be long remembered by the proud parents.

Recalling Facts

1. A baby spends his first year of life learning to
   - ☐ a. listen.
   - ☐ b. walk.
   - ☐ c. run.

2. The first sounds a child makes are called
   - ☐ a. comfort sounds.
   - ☐ b. discomfort sounds.
   - ☐ c. rhythm sounds.

3. The baby's comfort sounds appear around
   - ☐ a. one month.
   - ☐ b. three months.
   - ☐ c. six months.

4. Comfort sounds are
   - ☐ a. musical.
   - ☐ b. shrill.
   - ☐ c. throaty.

5. As the child gets older, he uses more
   - ☐ a. musical tones.
   - ☐ b. throaty sounds.
   - ☐ c. vowels and consonants.

Understanding the Passage

6. A baby learns how to listen before he learns how to
   - ☐ a. eat.
   - ☐ b. see.
   - ☐ c. talk.

7. Sound
   - ☐ a. can easily hurt a newborn baby.
   - ☐ b. means nothing to a newborn baby.
   - ☐ c. will put a newborn baby to sleep.

8. We can see that
   - ☐ a. children learn while they sleep.
   - ☐ b. the ears develop before the brain.
   - ☐ c. shrill whines show that the child is happy.

9. If you make a loud noise near a newborn baby, he seems to
   - ☐ a. get angry.
   - ☐ b. ignore it.
   - ☐ c. look away.

10. The child needs to practice his sound making in order to
    - ☐ a. listen.
    - ☐ b. sing.
    - ☐ c. speak.

All over the world people swim for fun. Swimming is enjoyed by people of all ages, from the very young to the very old. There are many places for people to swim. People swim in lakes, oceans, and rivers. Some swim in pools. Many schools, motels, apartment buildings, and clubs have indoor or outdoor pools. There are some folks who have pools in their yards.

Swimming is one of the best forms of exercise. It can improve heart action. It also helps blood circulate. Swimming will develop strong muscles. It will even strengthen the lungs. People who are handicapped and can't enjoy other sports can keep their bodies in better condition by ● swimming. It is a good idea for parents to see to it that their children learn to swim at an early age. This will be an activity that the children can enjoy for the rest of their lives.

There are many basic rules for water safety that can help save your life. These rules can also help you save the life of a friend.

First of all, know how to swim. Many schools give lessons to children as part of their athletic program. Adults can learn to swim at public pools ● or other recreation centers.

Another rule to remember is never swim alone. Always swim with a friend and know where that person is in the water at all times. It is best to swim only in places where there is a lifeguard. If you swim in the ocean or a river, it is good to know about tides and currents.

Whether you are a beginner or an experienced swimmer, it is good to know survival bobbing. This can help you if there is an accident. Survival bobbing lets you float for a long time on your stomach. This bobbing uses ● very little energy. You fill your lungs with air. At the same time, relax your body. Your arms and legs hang down limply and your chin flops down to your chest. The air in your lungs will hold your head above the water. When you need a breath, you breathe out through your nose. Next, lift your face out of the water and breathe in through your mouth. You then return to the restful floating position.

Never take dangerous chances when swimming. Most drownings could be avoided if everyone knew how to swim and followed the basic rules for water safety.

Recalling Facts

1. Swimming can improve
   - ☐ a. eyesight.
   - ☐ b. heart action.
   - ☐ c. personality.

2. Swimming develops strong
   - ☐ a. hands.
   - ☐ b. muscles.
   - ☐ c. teeth.

3. Many schools give swimming lessons to children as part of their
   - ☐ a. art program.
   - ☐ b. athletic program.
   - ☐ c. reading program.

4. If you swim in the ocean or a river, it is good to know about tides and
   - ☐ a. currents.
   - ☐ b. shorelines.
   - ☐ c. temperatures.

5. Whether you are a beginner or an experienced swimmer, it is good to know
   - ☐ a. back floating.
   - ☐ b. lifesaving.
   - ☐ c. survival bobbing.

Understanding the Passage

6. Swimming is an enjoyable
   - ☐ a. job.
   - ☐ b. sport.
   - ☐ c. talent.

7. This article hints that swimming is
   - ☐ a. good for the body.
   - ☐ b. not very much fun.
   - ☐ c. very dangerous.

8. Parents should
   - ☐ a. make sure their children can swim.
   - ☐ b. never take their children to the ocean.
   - ☐ c. not allow their children near water.

9. Swimming alone can be
   - ☐ a. dangerous.
   - ☐ b. helpful.
   - ☐ c. safe.

10. We can see that most drowning accidents could be avoided if people would
    - ☐ a. exercise regularly.
    - ☐ b. eat proper foods.
    - ☐ c. learn to swim.

When you buy new paint of high quality from a good store, it should be in excellent condition. First, stir the paint thoroughly, if it is a type that should be stirred. Then, look for lumps or curdling. Check to see that the colors have not separated. Do not use the paint if you see any of these signs.

When opened, old paints may give off a bad smell. This is sometimes true of latex paints. If the paint smells bad or shows signs of lumps, it should be thrown away and not used. You may find a "skin" on the paint when you open the can. Using a knife or paint stick, remove as much of this as you can. The paint will then have to be strained through cheese-cloth or fine wire mesh, such as window screening. If this is not done, bits of the skin will brush onto the work and spoil the paint job.

New paints should be ready for use when bought. Ask the salesperson at the store when you buy the paint about mixing. Be sure to read the label on the can. Some paints should not be mixed or stirred. If such paints are mixed, air bubbles may result. Paints that should be mixed can be done at the paint store. Most stores use a machine that shakes the can of paint for several minutes and mixes it thoroughly. You can mix the paint yourself at home using a paint stick. Ask the salesperson for a stick when you buy the paint.

Sometimes when you open a can of paint, you find that the pigment has settled. You will have to use a paint stick or a clean paddle to work the pigment up from the bottom. Use a strong, circular motion. Continue until the pigment is mixed well and the color is even. Check to be sure that there are no signs of color separation. If you find that the layer that has settled on the bottom is hard or rubbery, you may have to throw the can away. The paint is too old and cannot be used.

Make sure the can is tightly covered between paint jobs. If the air gets in, the paint will become thick and begin to dry out. If the lid is not tight, dust may get in. If the can is not completely covered, a skin may form.

Recalling Facts

1. Old paints can
   - ☐ a. explode.
   - ☐ b. peel.
   - ☐ c. smell bad.

2. Lumpy paint must be
   - ☐ a. mixed.
   - ☐ b. stored.
   - ☐ c. strained.

3. You can mix your own paint by using a
   - ☐ a. paint stick.
   - ☐ b. paint thinner.
   - ☐ c. spray painter.

4. When mixing paint, you should use a strong
   - ☐ a. back and forth motion.
   - ☐ b. circular motion.
   - ☐ c. up and down motion.

5. When air gets into the paint, it becomes
   - ☐ a. moldy.
   - ☐ b. thick.
   - ☐ c. thin.

Understanding the Passage

6. Curdled paint is
   - ☐ a. bright.
   - ☐ b. lumpy.
   - ☐ c. watery.

7. The "skin" on a can of paint is the
   - ☐ a. film that forms over the paint.
   - ☐ b. label that is on the can of paint.
   - ☐ c. type of lid that is on the can.

8. We can see that often it is not good to use
   - ☐ a. latex paint.
   - ☐ b. new paint.
   - ☐ c. old paint.

9. Some paint stores
   - ☐ a. make home deliveries.
   - ☐ b. mix the paint for you.
   - ☐ c. offer free paint samples.

10. When you finish using a can of paint, you should
    - ☐ a. make sure it is covered tightly.
    - ☐ b. remove the label on the can.
    - ☐ c. throw the left-over paint away.

Many animals have learned how to adjust to changes in their world. Some have learned how to live through cold winters when food is scarce. Their secret is a winter sleep called "hibernation." When temperatures drop, these animals go to sleep.

The best known hibernator is the bear. All bears can hibernate. But it is mainly those who live in the earth's colder lands that do.

Before a bear settles down for its long sleep, it stuffs itself with food. All bears like honey. They will do almost anything to get it. But they are almost as fond of berries. Berries help the bear put on that extra bit of fat it needs for its long winter sleep. In the late summer and early fall, ripe berries are plentiful. This is when the bear gets hungry. Bears will often travel as much as a hundred miles to feast among the berry bushes. Even the large bears like the grizzlies come down from the mountains to find berries.

It is true that bears hibernate during the winter because food is scarce. Yet, there is another reason for bears to take to the den during the cold months. This is the time when the cubs are born. Bear cubs, usually two to a litter, are tiny at birth compared to their mother. She may weigh as much as 600 to 800 pounds. Her cubs may weigh less than a pound apiece. The cubs are blind and helpless during the first few weeks after birth. In this state they could never survive an unfriendly winter. The winter den keeps the cubs safe and warm.

Bears' winter dens vary. The kind of den varies with the kind of bear and the climate it lives in. Some dens may be no more than a hole in a hollow stump. Some dens are mere holes dug in a river bank. The larger bears, however, need bigger dens. Grizzlies, for instance, dig out a den that is 10 to 12 feet deep. They bed it down with leaves. Then they seal it with earth and stones. Some bears in Yellowstone National Park even enjoy steam-heated caves among the hot springs. Black bears often build dens under a thick pile of logs. Or they may choose the roots of an upturned tree and let the heavy winter snows provide a good roof over them. Truly, hibernating keeps them safe and sound.

Recalling Facts

1. Animals hibernate during the
   - ☐ a. spring.
   - ☐ b. summer.
   - ☐ c. winter.

2. All bears like to eat
   - ☐ a. fish.
   - ☐ b. honey.
   - ☐ c. nuts.

3. How many bear cubs are usually in a litter?
   - ☐ a. one
   - ☐ b. two
   - ☐ c. three

4. An adult female bear weighs as much as
   - ☐ a. 100 to 200 pounds.
   - ☐ b. 600 to 800 pounds.
   - ☐ c. 900 to 1,200 pounds.

5. Grizzles dig out a den that is
   - ☐ a. 1 to 2 feet deep.
   - ☐ b. 5 to 8 feet deep.
   - ☐ c. 10 to 12 feet deep.

Understanding the Passage

6. We can guess that, if bears did not hibernate, they might
   - ☐ a. get lost in the woods.
   - ☐ b. starve to death.
   - ☐ c. trample their young.

7. A bear stuffs itself with food during the
   - ☐ a. winter and spring.
   - ☐ b. summer and fall.
   - ☐ c. fall and winter.

8. Bears get very fat
   - ☐ a. before they hibernate.
   - ☐ b. while they hibernate.
   - ☐ c. after they hibernate.

9. Bear cubs are born during the
   - ☐ a. spring.
   - ☐ b. summer.
   - ☐ c. winter.

10. Grizzlies are very
    - ☐ a. big.
    - ☐ b. slow.
    - ☐ c. small.

In order to teach a dog to come when he is called, the trainer must use a long rope. One end of the rope should be tied to the dog's collar. Then, he should be allowed to go away on his own. His name should be called along with the word "come." The rope should be jerked at the same time. The command should be repeated several times while the rope is being jerked. The lesson should be repeated until he obeys the command.

When the dog has learned to come when called, the lesson should be taught without the rope. If he does not come when he is called, the rope must be used again. This lesson should be repeated with and without the rope until he learns to come without it.

Another lesson is teaching the dog to walk on the left side of his trainer. A leash is needed for this lesson. The leash is held in the right hand.

The next step in this lesson is to say "heel." If the dog runs forward or lags behind, the leash should be jerked and the command should be repeated. Short, quick jerks are more effective than a continuous pull.

When the dog has learned to walk on the correct side, the lesson should be tried without the leash in an enclosed area. If the dog leaves, the leash should be put back on. The lesson should be repeated with and without the leash.

With the dog at heel position, he can learn how to sit. At the same time, his leash should be pulled back and his hips should be pushed down. This lesson can be repeated with the leash, and later without it, until he will sit on command.

The command "down" means lie down. In the sitting position, the dog is given the command. The leash should then be pulled down. At the same time his shoulders should be pushed gently. If he will not lie down this way, his front legs can be pulled forward until he lies down.

Dogs can be taught to stay in one place. The command "stay" is given while the dog is held in position. The trainer should then back away from him. If he moves, he should be put back in place. The lesson should be repeated until he will stay even when the trainer is out of his sight.

Recalling Facts

1. Training a dog to "heel" requires pulling the leash in
   - ☐ a. short, quick jerks.
   - ☐ b. long, continuous pulls.
   - ☐ c. strong, rapid tugs.

2. The author recommends using
   - ☐ a. an enclosed area.
   - ☐ b. a whip.
   - ☐ c. a chain.

3. The author discusses teaching a dog to walk
   - ☐ a. behind the trainer.
   - ☐ b. beside the trainer.
   - ☐ c. in front of the trainer.

4. According to the author, the leash should be fastened to the dog's
   - ☐ a. neck.
   - ☐ b. front paws.
   - ☐ c. collar.

5. A dog should learn to "stay" even when his trainer
   - ☐ a. offers food.
   - ☐ b. is out of sight.
   - ☐ c. is in danger.

Understanding the Passage

6. The author implies that the easiest lesson to teach is
   - ☐ a. "come."
   - ☐ b. "sit."
   - ☐ c. "down."

7. If a dog moves when he is being taught to stay, he must be
   - ☐ a. put back in place.
   - ☐ b. punished.
   - ☐ c. released.

8. In this article, the author shows how to
   - ☐ a. train a dog.
   - ☐ b. discipline a dog.
   - ☐ c. groom a dog.

9. The command "down" means
   - ☐ a. sit down.
   - ☐ b. roll over.
   - ☐ c. lie down.

10. If a dog refuses to follow the command "down,"
    - ☐ a. he should be rewarded before another attempt is made.
    - ☐ b. his front legs should be pulled forward.
    - ☐ c. he should not be fed for at least one day.

Minerals Make the Difference

Minerals are needed for a healthy body. They are needed to help our bodies grow. The most plentiful mineral in the body is calcium. Yet, it may not be found in many diets. Studies show that a lack of calcium may be found in all age groups. For instance, from the age of nine, the diets of girls and women may not have enough calcium. Their diets may lack as much as 25 to 30 percent of the calcium they need.

Almost all calcium is in bones and teeth. The rest is found in the tissue and body fluids. Calcium is needed for blood to clot. It is also needed for the heart to work properly. The nervous system does not work well when calcium levels in the blood are low. Even muscles work better when the body gets enough calcium.

Most people who buy from the milk counter are stocking up on calcium supplies. In the United States, we depend on milk as a big source of calcium. Two cups of milk, or an equal amount of cheese or other dairy products, gives us a lot of calcium. They go a long way toward giving us all the calcium needed for the day.

But milk is not the only source of calcium. Dark green leafy vegetables like collards, mustard greens, or turnip greens have calcium. Salmon and sardines give us useful amounts of it if the very tiny bones are eaten.

Calcium is not the only important mineral in the body. Iron is important, too. Women of childbearing age need more iron than men. The diets of infants and pregnant women may need to be watched closely to see that they have the iron they should.

Only a few foods have iron in large amounts. Liver, heart, kidney, and lean meats have a good deal of it. Shellfish, especially oysters, have a lot of iron. Whole grain and enriched breads and cereals are rich in iron. They give us up to one quarter of the daily iron we need. Dark green leafy vegetables are also sources of iron.

Calcium and iron are not the only minerals you need. Most of the other minerals your body needs are found in so many foods that a little variety in making your choice at the market can easily take care of them. Make a healthy, happy body your goal the next time you shop for food.

Recalling Facts

1. Calcium is a
   - ☐ a. fat.
   - ☐ b. mineral.
   - ☐ c. vitamin.

2. Almost all calcium is found in the bones and
   - ☐ a. hair.
   - ☐ b. nails.
   - ☐ c. teeth.

3. Calcium is needed to
   - ☐ a. carry waste.
   - ☐ b. clot blood.
   - ☐ c. fight infection.

4. A big source of calcium is
   - ☐ a. fat.
   - ☐ b. milk.
   - ☐ c. water.

5. Which of the following vegetables contains calcium?
   - ☐ a. collards
   - ☐ b. potatoes
   - ☐ c. squash

Understanding the Passage

6. What two minerals does this article talk about?
   - ☐ a. calcium and iron
   - ☐ b. iodine and calcium
   - ☐ c. potassium and sodium

7. What is the main idea of this article?
   - ☐ a. The body needs minerals in order to stay healthy.
   - ☐ b. Vegetables contain very few vitamins and minerals.
   - ☐ c. Vitamins are more important for a healthy body than minerals.

8. This article hints that many people
   - ☐ a. do not like foods that contain calcium.
   - ☐ b. lack enough calcium in their daily diets.
   - ☐ c. overcook their dark green leafy vegetables.

9. We can see that
   - ☐ a. infants need more iron than adult men.
   - ☐ b. pregnant women need very little iron.
   - ☐ c. women do not need as much iron as men.

10. Calcium seems to be needed mostly by
    - ☐ a. men.
    - ☐ b. infants.
    - ☐ c. women.

The time to plan for a fire emergency is before it happens. This is when everyone is calm and thinking clearly. This is when decisions about safe escape routes can be made and discussed. Have a family talk. Don't delay. Planning won't help after a fire starts.

Knowing ahead of time how to get out during a fire can save needed seconds. The best way out in a fire is the route you use to go in and out every day. Yet, in a fire this route may be blocked. Be sure to plan other escape routes.

Take each person to his or her room and describe what to do in case of fire. Give everyone a job. Older children should take care of younger ones. Plans may have to be made for anyone who cannot escape without help. Adults who can't walk should sleep on the first floor. Small children should sleep near older persons who can help them. Only healthy, able persons should sleep in hard-to-reach attics or basements.

Practice your escape plan at night when it is dark. Be sure that your plan is good and will work. For instance, make sure that a child can actually open the window he is supposed to use for his escape. Teach children to close their bedroom doors. Tell them to wait by an open window until someone can reach them from outside. If an adult cannot be wakened, children should understand that they must leave by themselves.

Choose a meeting place outside. This way you can tell if everyone is safely out of the building. Know where nearby telephones or fire alarm boxes are found.

If you live in an apartment, try to get everyone out. Learn where the fire alarm is in the building. Your family should know what the fire alarm bell or horn sounds like. They should know what to do when they hear it. Try to get the other families in your building together to have fire drills. Write down the telephone number of the fire department. Tape the number to each phone. Don't forget to let the babysitter in on your plans. Tell your babysitter what to do in case of fire.

Early warning is the key to a safe escape. It has been shown time and time again that a family can escape if warned early enough.

Recalling Facts

1. Before a fire breaks out, it's a good idea to plan your escape
   - ☐ a. clothes.
   - ☐ b. meals.
   - ☐ c. routes.

2. Adults who can't walk should sleep on the
   - ☐ a. first floor.
   - ☐ b. second floor.
   - ☐ c. third floor.

3. You should practice your escape plan at
   - ☐ a. noon.
   - ☐ b. dusk.
   - ☐ c. night.

4. Until someone can rescue a child, he should wait by the
   - ☐ a. bed.
   - ☐ b. open closet.
   - ☐ c. open window.

5. It's a good idea to write down the telephone number of the
   - ☐ a. family doctor.
   - ☐ b. fire department.
   - ☐ c. rescue squad.

Understanding the Passage

6. This article suggests that after a fire breaks out, people should be
   - ☐ a. calm.
   - ☐ b. confused.
   - ☐ c. quiet.

7. We can see that planning for a fire
   - ☐ a. can save lives.
   - ☐ b. is sometimes dangerous.
   - ☐ c. wastes a lot of time.

8. To be sure your escape plan works, you should
   - ☐ a. draw it.
   - ☐ b. practice it.
   - ☐ c. write it down.

9. If you are trapped in a bedroom during a fire, you should
   - ☐ a. close the bedroom door.
   - ☐ b. hide under the bed.
   - ☐ c. stand in a corner.

10. People who live in apartments should
    - ☐ a. have fire drills together.
    - ☐ b. make sure they know the fire chief.
    - ☐ c. not have to pay fire insurance.

Follow That Goose

Have you ever tracked a wild goose? Why would anyone want to? There is one kind of wild goose called the Emperor Goose. It is spied upon, followed, and watched. Every move that it makes is noticed and carefully written down. But don't feel sorry for the Emperor Goose. It's all for its own good.

Little is known about this goose. It is a North American waterfowl, and it is lovely and rare. Because this goose is so rare, researchers want to be sure that it will survive. To do this, they have to know and understand its habits.

The known nesting place of the Emperor Goose is small. It is found in a semi-wild part of the state of Alaska. The land around Kokechik Bay seems to attract the bird. The streams of the Yukon Delta empty into the bay. These same streams carry pollution to the nesting sites, especially after a storm. The researchers want to learn how people's actions affect the birds. First, we must know something about the goose itself.

To answer their questions, researchers have set up camps near the breeding grounds. After locating and studying the nests, scientists have learned many things. For example, they now know how the female guards her nest. She presses close to the ground. She stretches her neck out and remains quite still. In this way, she looks like a piece of driftwood. And who would bother with a piece of driftwood?

Scientists have also learned that after the Emperor Geese mate, they stay together. While the female sits on the eggs, the male stands or feeds nearby. At times, the male may wander off a little way. He is sure to come back quickly if the female is disturbed.

When the eggs hatch, the young geese are a dark gray color. After two weeks, the dark gray turns to a light gray. When the goslings reach the fledgling stage, they take on a blue tone. The adult goose can be recognized by the whiteness of its head and the back of its neck. This white contrasts with the black of its throat. The silver-gray feathers and its bright yellow-orange feet make this bird one of the most colorful of geese.

We need to know a lot more about the Emperor Goose. The researchers in Alaska hope to add to their knowledge in order to protect this amazing bird.

Recalling Facts

1. The Emperor Goose is a North American
   - ☐ a. amphibian.
   - ☐ b. reptile.
   - ☐ c. waterfowl.

2. What state does the Emperor Goose nest in?
   - ☐ a. Alaska
   - ☐ b. Iowa
   - ☐ c. Maine

3. When the female goose tries to protect her nest, she looks like a piece of
   - ☐ a. dirt.
   - ☐ b. driftwood.
   - ☐ c. rock.

4. The adult goose has a white
   - ☐ a. beak.
   - ☐ b. head.
   - ☐ c. throat.

5. What color feet does the Emperor Goose have?
   - ☐ a. gray-white
   - ☐ b. red-brown
   - ☐ c. yellow-orange

Understanding the Passage

6. Choose the best title for this article.
   - ☐ a. Alaska—the Wild Land
   - ☐ b. All about the Emperor Goose
   - ☐ c. A Trip to Canada

7. This article suggests that the Emperor Goose is
   - ☐ a. fierce.
   - ☐ b. large.
   - ☐ c. scarce.

8. We can see that researchers have learned much about the goose's
   - ☐ a. eating habits.
   - ☐ b. nesting habits.
   - ☐ c. sleeping habits.

9. Where is the Yukon?
   - ☐ a. near the equator
   - ☐ b. in the Northern Hemisphere
   - ☐ c. in the Southern Hemisphere

10. As the Emperor Goose grows from a baby to an adult, it changes its
    - ☐ a. color.
    - ☐ b. diet.
    - ☐ c. personality.

Almost all foods give us energy. Some give us more energy than others. Energy is measured in calories. Foods rich in fats, starches, or sugars have a lot of calories. Fat is a big source of energy.

At times you eat foods that have more energy, or calories, than you need. The extra energy is then stored in the body as fat. If you eat too much, you become overweight. When you eat fewer calories than the body uses, you lose weight.

The body can pick and choose what it needs from the nutrients in the diet. Your body sees to it that each organ gets exactly the right amount of nutrients it needs. However, if the diet lacks some of the needed nutrients, the body has no way of getting them.

Your body keeps busy. It works twenty-four hours a day. It is always building itself up, repairing itself, and getting rid of waste products. It needs a constant supply of nutrients to do its job. When it receives the nutrients, it sends them where they are needed.

Let's take calcium as an example. The body needs calcium. Calcium helps to clot blood. It also helps build bones. Calcium helps make the nerves and muscles work well. If your body does not get enough calcium from the food you eat, it steals some from your bones. If the stolen calcium is not replaced, the body is in trouble. You may not realize this fact for some years. As much as one-third of the normal amount of calcium may be taken from an adult's bones before the loss shows up on an X-ray film.

Nutrients working with other nutrients make the difference in our health and well-being. No single nutrient can work properly alone. For example, it takes calcium to build strong bones, but that is only the beginning. Without vitamin D, the calcium cannot be taken into the body. The use of protein is another example. Protein forms part of every cell and all the fluids that travel in and around the cells. However, it takes vitamin C to help make the fluids between the cells. Without vitamin C, the protein could not do its job.

The foods you eat keep you healthy for today, but they also build your body for a lifetime. They keep you well today, tomorrow, and always.

Recalling Facts

1. Energy is measured in
   - ☐ a. calories.
   - ☐ b. pounds.
   - ☐ c. watts.

2. Which of these is a big source of energy?
   - ☐ a. fats
   - ☐ b. vegetables
   - ☐ c. water

3. If you eat too much, you become
   - ☐ a. active.
   - ☐ b. graceful.
   - ☐ c. overweight.

4. Calcium helps to build
   - ☐ a. bones.
   - ☐ b. calories.
   - ☐ c. fluids.

5. Protein forms part of every
   - ☐ a. cell.
   - ☐ b. nutrient.
   - ☐ c. vitamin.

Understanding the Passage

6. Our energy comes from the
   - ☐ a. clothes we wear.
   - ☐ b. foods we eat.
   - ☐ c. water we drink.

7. This article hints that, in order to work properly, your body needs
   - ☐ a. electricity.
   - ☐ b. nutrients.
   - ☐ c. tobacco.

8. We can see that our body contains a good amount of
   - ☐ a. protein.
   - ☐ b. fat.
   - ☐ c. X-rays.

9. Without calcium, our bones would become very
   - ☐ a. damp.
   - ☐ b. strong.
   - ☐ c. weak.

10. What is the main idea of this article?
    - ☐ a. The foods we eat keep us healthy.
    - ☐ b. Our bodies need daily exercise.
    - ☐ c. Protein is not always good for us.

39 Watch Your Trigger Finger

An electric drill can do many jobs. With it you can make holes in almost anything. By using its attachments, you can sand, polish, grind, and buff. You can even stir paint. Plus you can drive screws with it.

The cost of a drill depends on its size, quality, and special features. Many cost under $50. It is best to choose a type of drill that has the features you will use often.

The work capacity of a drill depends on two things. It depends on the drill's revolutions per minute (RPM). The chuck size of a drill is the diameter of the largest bit shank the drill chuck can hold. Home-use sizes are one-fourth, three-eighths, and one-half inch. As a rule, the larger the chuck, the wider and deeper the holes the drill makes. The RPM rating tells you the speed and type of work the drill is best suited for. For instance, a ¼-inch drill rated about 2,000 RPM usually has one gear. It is good for rapid drilling in wood. It can also be used with sanding and polishing attachments. A model with more gears has a lower RPM rating and would work more slowly. But this drill could make bigger holes in hard surfaces without stalling or overheating.

For most jobs around the home, use a single-speed drill. However, a two-speed model would be better if you plan to drill something that needs a slow speed.

Most drills have a pistol-grip handle. The handle should be well balanced and comfortable. It should have fingerholds in front. The fingerholds stop your hand from slipping. Some models also have side handles which may be attached so that the drill can be grasped by both hands. These handles are good for heavy work or if the drill is held in an awkward position.

A trigger switch starts the drill and is found on the pistol-grip handle. Some drills also have a switch lock. You set the lock by pressing the button. The lock should release instantly if you tighten your squeeze on the trigger switch. This lock is used when the drill runs for a long period of time.

Variable-speed drills have trigger switches that let you change the speed of the drill just by using trigger-finger pressure. This type of drill gives you better control than other drills. Control while drilling is vital for safety and for performance.

Recalling Facts

1. An electric drill can sand, polish, grind, and
   - ☐ a. buff.
   - ☐ b. saw.
   - ☐ c. sort.

2. The cost of a drill depends on its size, quality, and
   - ☐ a. carrying case.
   - ☐ b. special features.
   - ☐ c. wattage.

3. Many drills cost under
   - ☐ a. $15.
   - ☐ b. $25.
   - ☐ c. $50.

4. A ¼-inch drill rated about 2,000 RPM usually has
   - ☐ a. one gear.
   - ☐ b. two gears.
   - ☐ c. three gears.

5. The handle of a drill should be well balanced and
   - ☐ a. comfortable.
   - ☐ b. dirty.
   - ☐ c. pretty.

Understanding the Passage

6. We can see that electric drills
   - ☐ a. can be used for many jobs.
   - ☐ b. make painting an easy job.
   - ☐ c. use a lot of electricity.

7. Drills are not very
   - ☐ a. dependable.
   - ☐ b. expensive.
   - ☐ c. useful.

8. What kind of hole can you drill with a large chuck?
   - ☐ a. deep and wide
   - ☐ b. long and narrow
   - ☐ c. wide and short

9. A ¼-inch drill is good for
   - ☐ a. cutting through stone.
   - ☐ b. drilling through metal.
   - ☐ c. sanding a table.

10. You can change the speed on a variable-speed drill by changing the pressure on the
    - ☐ a. bit.
    - ☐ b. cord.
    - ☐ c. trigger.

How Animals Defend Themselves

All animals are constantly struggling to keep their own kind alive. This battle is sometimes called the "struggle for survival." Animals that are alive today have won this battle. But many have lost the battle in the past. And many will lose it in the future. Dinosaurs and other ancient animals vanished long ago. Other animals died out in more recent times. In this century, these extinct animals include the heath hen, the West Indian seal, and the passenger pigeon.

The kinds of animals that live today have achieved useful ways of surviving. Every kind of animal can defend itself in some way. An attack might come from some other animal hunting for food. Or an attack may come from humans hunting for sport. Some animals hide when in danger. Their color or shape keeps them from being seen. Animals that rely on their color for protection have a unique protective coloration. For example, a white polar bear seems to vanish in the snow. Animals that depend on their shape to help them hide have protective resemblance. The praying mantis has a long body and leaflike wings. It looks like a torn leaf when it stands still.

A few kinds of animals try to "play dead" when an enemy comes near. The opossum is famous for playing dead. If it is harmed, it closes its eyes and lets its body go limp. This animal stays that way even if it is dropped, turned over, or picked up.

Several types of animals have built-in armor to protect them. Some have a shell of hard covering. Others have sharp quills or spines.

Clams, conches, and snails pull back into their shells and keep them shut until danger passes. The porcupine has sharp quills that have barbs like fish hooks. This animal humps its back when attacked. The quills then stick out in all directions.

Most animals try to flee from their enemies. The deer, horse, antelope, kangaroo, and ostrich can usually outrun their foes. Most birds take to the air when they feel threatened. Most kinds of animals will fight when cut off from flight. The lion and other members of the cat family fight with sharp claws and strong teeth. Moose, deer, and elk kick their enemies and also use their antlers as weapons. But fighting is usually the last resort for most animals. Unlike humans, most animals are not aggressive in nature.

Recalling Facts

1. The "battle for survival" has been
   - ☐ a. won by all animals in the past.
   - ☐ b. lost by the heath hen.
   - ☐ c. won by the West Indian seal.

2. What is the least used method of animal defense?
   - ☐ a. flight from danger
   - ☐ b. fighting with the enemy
   - ☐ c. "playing dead"

3. Protective coloration is a
   - ☐ a. method of animal survival.
   - ☐ b. type of oil painting.
   - ☐ c. form of defense used by the opossum.

4. Protective resemblance is a form of defense used by
   - ☐ a. the polar bear.
   - ☐ b. the praying mantis.
   - ☐ c. dinosaurs.

5. Which type of bird does not fly in moments of danger?
   - ☐ a. the ostrich
   - ☐ b. the robin
   - ☐ c. the sparrow

Understanding the Passage

6. Certain defenses enable animals to
   - ☐ a. lose the "struggle for survival."
   - ☐ b. win the "struggle for survival."
   - ☐ c. live forever.

7. When threatened, most animals can be
   - ☐ a. dangerous.
   - ☐ b. friendly.
   - ☐ c. harmless.

8. Many attacks upon animals come from
   - ☐ a. young animals playing.
   - ☐ b. humans hunting for sport.
   - ☐ c. smaller animals fighting for their territory.

9. What is the main idea of this selection?
   - ☐ a. the extinction of dinosaurs
   - ☐ b. the survival of fish in the sea
   - ☐ c. successful ways of animal defense

10. A good title of this selection would be
   - ☐ a. Why Humans Hunt.
   - ☐ b. Why Animals Fight.
   - ☐ c. Why Animals Survive.

Vitamins are important to our bodies. They keep our bodies healthy. They help our bodies to grow. There are at least 25 different vitamins we know of. Each one has its own special use. The best way to get vitamins is to eat foods rich in them. It's a good idea, then, to know about foods and the vitamins they contain. Let's take a look at four special vitamins. We can start with vitamin A.

Vitamin A is needed for good eyesight. It helps us to see better at night. It even keeps our eyes free from disease. Vitamin A also keeps the skin healthy and stops infection. This vitamin is found in animal foods. However, deep yellow and dark green vegetables and fruits give our bodies something called "carotene." Our bodies can turn carotene into vitamin A.

Produce can easily supply all the vitamin A you need. Such items as collards, turnip greens, kale, carrots, squash, and sweet potatoes can more than take care of daily needs. Yellow peaches, apricots, cantaloupe, and papayas also help.

Liver is another good source of vitamin A. A two-ounce serving of cooked beef liver gives us more than 30,000 units of the vitamin. That's six times more vitamin A than you would need during the day.

There are plenty of other sources of vitamin A. Whole milk is a source. Skim milk, on the other hand, doesn't have any vitamin A, unless it is fortified. This means that vitamin A has been added to it.

Three of the best known vitamins come from the vitamin B complex. They are riboflavin, thiamine and niacin. These vitamins release the energy in food. They keep the nervous system working. They keep the digestive system working calmly. And they even help to keep the skin healthy.

Riboflavin is easy to find. It is found in meats, milk, and whole grain or enriched breads. Organ meats also have riboflavin.

Thiamine is found in few foods. Lean pork is one. Dry beans and peas and some of the organ meats also have thiamine.

Niacin can be found in whole grain and enriched cereals. Meat and meat products and peas and beans also contain niacin. Without niacin, riboflavin and thiamine could not do their work properly.

Vitamins are very important to a healthy body. It is important to learn more about these amazing building blocks.

Recalling Facts

1. Vitamins help keep our bodies
   - ☐ a. healthy.
   - ☐ b. tan.
   - ☐ c. weak.

2. Vitamin A is needed for good
   - ☐ a. bones.
   - ☐ b. energy.
   - ☐ c. eyesight.

3. Deep yellow and dark green vegetables give our bodies
   - ☐ a. calcium.
   - ☐ b. carotene.
   - ☐ c. fat.

4. Which of the following is a good source of vitamin A?
   - ☐ a. liver
   - ☐ b. sugar
   - ☐ c. water

5. Thiamine is found in
   - ☐ a. enriched cereals.
   - ☐ b. lean pork.
   - ☐ c. whole milk.

Understanding the Passage

6. What is this article mostly about?
   - ☐ a. fats, protein, sugar, and starches
   - ☐ b. vitamins A, B, C, and D
   - ☐ c. vitamin A, riboflavin, thiamine, and niacin

7. To help us see better at night, we should eat
   - ☐ a. cabbage.
   - ☐ b. candy.
   - ☐ c. squash.

8. About how many units of vitamin A do we need a day?
   - ☐ a. 1,000
   - ☐ b. 5,000
   - ☐ c. 30,000

9. Some organ meats are rich in vitamin A and
   - ☐ a. calcium.
   - ☐ b. riboflavin.
   - ☐ c. vitamin K.

10. This article suggests that riboflavin, thiamine, and niacin
    - ☐ a. build bones.
    - ☐ b. tone muscles.
    - ☐ c. work together.

Watching Your Stepladder

The stepladder and the extension ladder are two types of ladders. They are used mostly around the home. They are made of many kinds of materials. They also come in many styles. You should choose the ladder you need for the job at hand.

A stepladder is self-supporting. It is also easy to carry. The only problem with a stepladder is that the length is fixed. Even so, stepladders are useful for many indoor jobs where the height to be reached is low. Just make sure the ladder can be placed on a firm, level surface.

The steps of your stepladder should be flat. They should be parallel and level when the ladder is open. Also, steps should be coated with a non-skid material. The space between steps should not be more than 12 inches. The depth of the step should be from 2½ to three inches. The steps should not be dented or bent. There should be no sharp edges. The bottom step should always be braced with metal angle braces.

The locking device on a stepladder should be large and strong. Your ladder should be rustproof. If you use your ladder for painting, make sure the bucket shelf can hold 25 pounds. It should fold with the ladder.

An extension ladder differs from a stepladder. It is straight and does not have a fixed length. It is made of two or more straight sections which travel in guides.

Each section of an extension ladder should overlap the next section by three or four feet, depending on length. A sixty-foot ladder should have an overlap of five feet. This kind of ladder should have safety stops. These stops will not let the ladder open too far.

Since ladders can be rather expensive, they should be cared for. They should not be stored outside. Wood ladders should be kept in a place where there is plenty of air. Do not place them close to dampness or high heat. Extension ladders should be stored in flat racks or on wall hangers. If long ladders are stored standing up, they may weaken and sag.

Cracked or rotten rungs of wood ladders should be repaired by a good repair shop. Don't do it yourself unless you have experience and the tools to do the job right. Having a ladder that is in good working condition is important for safety reasons.

*Reading Time*_____ *Comprehension Score*_____ *Words per Minute*_____

Recalling Facts

1. A stepladder is easy to
   □ a. carry.
   □ b. clean.
   □ c. replace.

2. The problem with a
   stepladder is that the
   □ a. edges are sharp.
   □ b. length is fixed.
   □ c. rungs are round.

3. The steps of your stepladder
   should be
   □ a. flat.
   □ b. round.
   □ c. square.

4. The space between the steps
   on a ladder should not be
   more than
   □ a. 5 inches.
   □ b. 12 inches.
   □ c. 16 inches.

5. Your ladder should be
   □ a. colorful.
   □ b. expensive.
   □ c. rustproof.

Understanding the Passage

6. Most stepladders are used
   □ a. in the home.
   □ b. along the seashore.
   □ c. around the yard.

7. A stepladder could be used to
   □ a. reach a high shelf in
         a cabinet.
   □ b. repair a broken roof vent.
   □ c. roof a house.

8. If a ladder is not placed on a firm
   surface, it might become
   □ a. shaky.
   □ b. slippery.
   □ c. rusty.

9. We can see that dampness can
   damage ladders that are made of
   □ a. plastic.
   □ b. stone.
   □ c. wood.

10. This article suggests that it's not a
    good idea to
    □ a. buy a wooden stepladder.
    □ b. loan your ladder to a friend.
    □ c. repair a ladder yourself.

43 Happy Birthday to You

What do the candles on your birthday cake mean? They simply tell your age. That's all. They don't tell what kind of jobs you can do. They don't say how healthy you are. Yet, your age has become a figure that can control your life. Your income, your social benefits, and your way of life greatly depend upon your age.

Yet a person's "calendar" age may not be a good measurement to use. You may be sixty-five years old by the calendar. Still you may feel and act even younger than a person who is fifty-five.

As a result, employers today are starting to depend more on "functional" age. The actual date of birth is becoming less of a factor. Older workers have a great deal to offer a company. They are wiser, more experienced and use better judgment than new employees. As a rule, they know how to make a decision and when to make it. They know when to speak up and when not to. Most important, they probably know when to listen, something that is usually not seen before middle age.

History tells us of people who reached their peak after middle age. Verdi wrote "Othello" when he was seventy-three. Cervantes wrote *Don Quixote* when in his middle years. Ben Franklin invented bifocal lenses when he was in his seventies.

Pearl Buck, a great writer, once talked about her eightieth birthday. She said that she was a far better person at eighty than she was at fifty or forty. She said that she had learned a great deal since she was seventy. She felt that she had learned more in those ten years than in any other ten-year period.

In fact, Pearl Buck was right. Studies show that smart people tend to get smarter as they grow older. The brain is like a muscle. The more you use it, the more it develops. Each one of us has something that can be used to help society and ourselves.

By working to develop the inherent good qualities each one of us possesses, we can strengthen and improve our skills. Many people think that old age is a cue to simply do nothing. Studies have shown that physical as well as mental exercise improves health and well-being in the later years of life. Don't let the candles on a birthday cake stand in the way.

Recalling Facts

1. Your age often controls your
   - ☐ a. family.
   - ☐ b. friends.
   - ☐ c. income.

2. Employers today depend more on a person's
   - ☐ a. actual age.
   - ☐ b. functional age.
   - ☐ c. spouse's age.

3. Who wrote "Othello"?
   - ☐ a. Cervantes
   - ☐ b. Plato
   - ☐ c. Verdi

4. Franklin invented bifocal lenses when he was in his
   - ☐ a. forties.
   - ☐ b. fifties.
   - ☐ c. seventies.

5. Pearl Buck was a famous
   - ☐ a. doctor.
   - ☐ b. lawyer.
   - ☐ c. writer.

Understanding the Passage

6. What would be another good title for this article?
   - ☐ a. Famous Scientists in History
   - ☐ b. The History of Birthday Cakes
   - ☐ c. You Don't Act Your Age

7. What is the main idea of this article?
   - ☐ a. Some older people have interesting hobbies.
   - ☐ b. Many older people act younger than their ages.
   - ☐ c. Most older people retire when they reach sixty-five.

8. Employers are finding out that older workers are
   - ☐ a. good for the company.
   - ☐ b. poor decision makers.
   - ☐ c. quite sickly.

9. We can see that many people invent things
   - ☐ a. after their middle years.
   - ☐ b. before they go to college.
   - ☐ c. quite often by accident.

10. Often, the older you get, the
   - ☐ a. happier you become.
   - ☐ b. shorter you become.
   - ☐ c. smarter you become.

Stand on Your Own Two Feet

A resourceful child is one who learns over the years to stand on her own two feet. She will find life easier. She will be able to find new solutions when faced with problems. Child experts have learned that there are ways to help a child become more resourceful.

Also, a child grows best when she has a chance to see the world around her. A child needs to have many kinds of experiences. She can take trips to the park, the store, the playground, the zoo, the fire station, or a pet shop. There are many safe places a child can explore.

A child should learn to speak for herself. When the dentist, waiter, or storekeeper speaks to a child, she should be allowed to give her own reply. A child should be allowed to run errands that are safe. Let a child carry a letter to a neighbor or pick up the mail.

A parent should give the child enough help to make the child feel comfortable. A parent should not, of course, push a child. Shyness cannot be forced away. Children should not be asked to speak up when they are better off being quiet. A child should not be put into a situation where she would feel ill at ease.

A parent should let his child make decisions. When she does, she finds out about choices. She learns what it is like to make a choice and to live with it. Parents can help by finding times when children can make choices and decide things. For example, there are times when youngsters can help to plan their own activities. To help children, keep the choices simple.

When children are three, four, five, and six years old, they delight in proving how grown-up they are. Giving children small jobs in the home makes them feel helpful. Most homes have many kinds of tools that a child can use. For example, a four-year-old can use a sponge or a dust cloth. A five-year-old can handle a hammer and saw, with adult help. A six-year-old can take snapshots at Christmas. These children will know they are needed. This is a first big step to becoming self-confident and resourceful.

Once a child feels comfortable with and confident in her abilities, she will be able to tackle larger projects.

Recalling Facts

1. A child that can stand on her own two feet is
   - ☐ a. gloomy.
   - ☐ b. shy.
   - ☐ c. resourceful.

2. According to this article, a five-year-old can handle
   - ☐ a. an adding machine.
   - ☐ b. a hammer and saw.
   - ☐ c. a simple camera.

3. A child should be allowed to run errands that are
   - ☐ a. harmful.
   - ☐ b. safe.
   - ☐ c. unplanned.

4. In order to teach self-confidence, a parent should let his child make
   - ☐ a. decisions.
   - ☐ b. mistakes.
   - ☐ c. noise.

5. When helping children plan their own activities, the choices should be
   - ☐ a. confusing.
   - ☐ b. difficult.
   - ☐ c. simple.

Understanding the Passage

6. What is the main idea of this article?
   - ☐ a. Children can learn to be resourceful.
   - ☐ b. Children can learn to read at an early age.
   - ☐ c. Shy children are usually unhappy.

7. Many children take their first big step to becoming self-confident between the ages of
   - ☐ a. one and two.
   - ☐ b. three and five.
   - ☐ c. eight and ten.

8. Shy children should
   - ☐ a. be asked to speak up.
   - ☐ b. be scolded.
   - ☐ c. not be pushed.

9. We can see that letting a child perform simple tasks makes her feel
   - ☐ a. angry and upset.
   - ☐ b. sad and shy.
   - ☐ c. wanted and loved.

10. A confident child is
    - ☐ a. better able to solve life's problems.
    - ☐ b. more apt to shy away from trouble.
    - ☐ c. usually a follower and not a leader.

What is the best wood to burn in the home fireplace? Choosing the kind of wood to burn is like choosing a bottle of wine. Each choice you can make has something different to offer. Woods differ in the scent they give off and in the heat they provide. The kind of wood you will choose depends on your own needs and tastes.

Pine, spruce, and fir are soft and easy to light. They burn quickly with a hot flame. However, a fire built from these woods burns out quickly. This kind of fire requires a lot of attention. It needs new logs added to keep the fire burning. A fire built from softwoods might be ideal for you at certain times. You may want a quick warming fire that will burn out before you go to bed.

For a long-lasting fire, it is best to use heavier woods. These would be ash, beech, birch, maple, and oak. These woods don't burn as fast. Oak gives the most even and shortest flames. It also produces steady, glowing coals. When you have several oak logs burning in your grate, you can settle back for a steady show of flame.

If you want a good-smelling fire, use the wood from fruit trees. Apple, cherry, and nut trees all produce pleasant scents. Their smoke usually smells like the tree's fruit.

By mixing softwoods with hardwoods, you can get a long-lasting, easy-to-light fire. Later, by adding some fruitwood, you can produce a pleasant scent as well.

As a rule, no more than four logs are needed to make a good fire. Adjust the logs to maintain the flames. Push the ends of the logs into the flames from time to time. Add kindling and new logs as needed to rekindle a dying flame. Rake coals toward the front of the grate before adding new logs and put new logs at the rear. There they will reflect light and heat into the room.

Let only an inch or two of ash collect at the bottom of the grate. Any more than this can ruin the andirons. Too much ash blocks the flow of air to the fire. Some ash is needed to form a bed for the glowing coals that drop through the grate. They help to hold the heat and direct drafts of air up to the base of the fire.

Recalling Facts

1. The kind of wood you burn in your fireplace depends on your own taste and
   - ☐ a. budget.
   - ☐ b. needs.
   - ☐ c. personality.

2. Pine is a
   - ☐ a. fruitwood.
   - ☐ b. hardwood.
   - ☐ c. softwood.

3. Spruce burns with a
   - ☐ a. cold flame.
   - ☐ b. hot flame.
   - ☐ c. short flame.

4. If you want a good-smelling fire, use the wood from
   - ☐ a. evergreen trees.
   - ☐ b. fruit trees.
   - ☐ c. oak trees.

5. How many logs are needed to make a good fire?
   - ☐ a. four
   - ☐ b. eight
   - ☐ c. ten

Understanding the Passage

6. What is the main idea of this article?
   - ☐ a. Fruitwood does not burn well in a fireplace.
   - ☐ b. Wet wood is easily dried in a home fireplace.
   - ☐ c. You should choose your fireplace wood carefully.

7. If you want a fire to last a long time, you should burn
   - ☐ a. oak.
   - ☐ b. pine.
   - ☐ c. spruce.

8. Burning cherry wood smells like
   - ☐ a. cherries.
   - ☐ b. dry leaves.
   - ☐ c. roses.

9. In order to get more heat out of your fireplace, you should
   - ☐ a. add new logs to the back of the fire.
   - ☐ b. clean your chimney once a year.
   - ☐ c. rake coals toward the rear of the fireplace.

10. A big ash buildup on the grate can
    - ☐ a. cause a fire.
    - ☐ b. damage the andirons.
    - ☐ c. stop up the chimney.

Do you know what to do if someone you know has a drug problem? The best thing is to stop drug abuse before it starts. But sometimes someone you know and care about can get involved with drugs. If that happens, don't panic or get angry. This won't help either one of you. Your friend needs your help and understanding more than ever before.

Solving an existing drug problem is called intervention. In some ways intervention is like prevention. You need to know what your friend is going through. Keep in mind the reasons people use drugs. They want to change the way they feel. They want to get away from a problem. Drug abuse is often a sign of another problem. Your friend may be hurt, angry, or upset. He or she may have begun to use drugs because of peer pressure. The first step, then, is to try to find out what the problem is. Talk to your friend. Be open and calm. Almost any problem can be talked about. Listen to each other. Don't cut each other off.

If your friend has a bad drug problem that the two of you can't handle, get help. Don't try to handle a crisis or medical emergency alone. Nearly every town has hot lines, counselors, and groups that can help. They can give you the help you need without getting you or your friend in trouble. Many schools now have drug counseling services. If your school doesn't, maybe you can urge the principal to start such a program. Also, don't forget about your parents. Drug problems are something most young people would rather not discuss with their parents. But drug problems are like a lot of other problems. Parents have helped their children get through other problems while growing up. Perhaps they can help with a drug problem, too.

The last thing to know is that helping a friend with a drug problem works best when it's done early. Long-term use is more likely to hurt you or your friend. If you think a friend has a drug problem, act quickly but calmly. You can make the difference.

Drug abuse is a problem which can be prevented. Prevention is not easy, but it is a simple idea. You may already be doing prevention now. Be a friend. Stop drug abuse before it starts.

Recalling Facts

1. If your friend becomes involved in drugs, you should not
   - ☐ a. listen.
   - ☐ b. panic.
   - ☐ c. talk.

2. Solving an existing drug problem is called
   - ☐ a. convention.
   - ☐ b. intervention.
   - ☐ c. prevention.

3. Some people use drugs to get away from
   - ☐ a. home.
   - ☐ b. other people.
   - ☐ c. a problem.

4. Some people use drugs because of pressure from their
   - ☐ a. doctors.
   - ☐ b. peers.
   - ☐ c. teachers.

5. If your friend has a bad drug problem that you can't handle, then you should
   - ☐ a. forget it.
   - ☐ b. get help.
   - ☐ c. hide it.

Understanding the Passage

6. This article is about
   - ☐ a. drug abuse.
   - ☐ b. drug counseling services.
   - ☐ c. medical emergencies.

7. The best way to stop a drug problem is to
   - ☐ a. get angry at your friend.
   - ☐ b. stop it before it starts.
   - ☐ c. tell the person's parents.

8. What should you do if your friend has a drug problem?
   - ☐ a. Remain calm and try to help.
   - ☐ b. Report your friend to the police.
   - ☐ c. Take your friend to a doctor.

9. What does this article hint at?
   - ☐ a. Adults often use drugs given to them by the doctor.
   - ☐ b. Kids don't like to talk about their drug problems with parents.
   - ☐ c. Some people have a bad reaction to some drugs.

10. We can see that
    - ☐ a. drugs are not as harmful as people think.
    - ☐ b. stopping a drug problem is not easy.
    - ☐ c. teachers often report students for using drugs.

A baby spends her first year in a pre-language state. She is learning how to listen. A baby spends her second year in a pre-speech state. She is learning how to talk. This begins when she starts to notice that certain sounds stand for certain objects. Her actions show this. When a baby hears the sound of a voice, she starts jabbering. When she hears the sound of scolding, she frowns. A baby cries when she hears thunder. She becomes quiet at the sound of her mother working around the house.

By her twelfth month, a baby can understand some words. If her father asks, "Show me the cup," the baby looks at or points to the cup. About the time she is a year-and-a-half old, the child seems to stretch her hearing skills. She will pay attention to sounds that come from far away. These are sounds from another room or from outdoors that she ignored before. At this age some children can recognize parts of their bodies. Say "nose" and they point to their nose; say "mouth" and they touch their mouth. They still need your gestures to help them understand what you say.

For most parents the greatest event in their child's second year is her first word. But just because a child makes the sound "mamamama" doesn't mean that she is using the sound to mean her mother. She must actually say the sound with a thought in mind before you can be really sure. Not until "mama" means "Mother, come here" is she using the sound in the sense of a tool.

The first words a child uses are usually commands or the names of something she recognizes. "Mum" may mean "I want milk." "Goggie" may mean "I see a dog." These early words are not pronounced well. Almost always they are the sounds that she can make easily. Many of these sounds have a very general meaning. "Goggie" can mean a dog, a cat, a stuffed lion, or a horse. As time goes on, the child learns to see the differences among these objects. She begins to learn the real names for each of them. When she puts names and objects together, the child is not only learning how to talk, but also how to think.

It may seem like this is a long process, but before the age of one, a baby learns faster than she will in her entire life.

Recalling Facts

1. A baby spends her first year in a
   - ☐ a. pre-growth state.
   - ☐ b. pre-language state.
   - ☐ c. pre-speech state.

2. During the second year, a baby learns how to
   - ☐ a. listen.
   - ☐ b. sit.
   - ☐ c. talk.

3. Babies can understand some words by their
   - ☐ a. first month.
   - ☐ b. fifth month.
   - ☐ c. twelfth month.

4. At what age can some children recognize parts of their body?
   - ☐ a. at three months
   - ☐ b. at six months
   - ☐ c. at one and a half years

5. the first words a child uses are usually the words of a
   - ☐ a. command.
   - ☐ b. statement.
   - ☐ c. question.

Understanding the Passage

6. We can see that children learn how to
   - ☐ a. crawl before they sit.
   - ☐ b. listen before they speak.
   - ☐ c. speak before they think.

7. This article hints that babies
   - ☐ a. do not hear soft and low sounds.
   - ☐ b. get into many unusual places.
   - ☐ c. react to the sounds around them.

8. Babies can understand before they can
   - ☐ a. roll over.
   - ☐ b. sit.
   - ☐ c. talk.

9. When a baby says her first word, she may not always
   - ☐ a. be able to whisper.
   - ☐ b. mean what she says.
   - ☐ c. try to repeat it.

10. A child's first word may
    - ☐ a. be clear and forceful.
    - ☐ b. be spoken in a whisper.
    - ☐ c. not be well pronounced.

Loud noises can affect your hearing. They can cause ear pain. Even worse, if sound waves from very loud noises reach your inner ear, they can rip and tear tissues needed for hearing.

Often ears will heal themselves if they are not hurt too badly. There may only be a short time after the loud noise that you cannot hear. But hearing can be lost forever if the damage is very bad. Or hearing may be damaged so that you may hear some sounds, but not others. For example, a car horn may be heard, but you may not be able to hear someone speaking.

It is a sad fact, but the world is getting noisier. Big machines roar, air conditioners whir, lawn mowers snarl, horns blast, sirens screech, telephones ring, people yell, and dogs bark. Noise is just about everywhere. Yet, our world could be made quieter. Every effort should be made to do away with loud noise. Our health depends upon it.

One way to cut down on noise is to quiet the thing that makes the noise. For instance, mufflers on car exhaust pipes cut down on the amount of noise a car makes. Without mufflers you could hardly stand the noise of your own car. That is one reason why mufflers are important.

Noise can also be stopped in other ways. One way is to soak up noise. Sound waves bounce off walls and ceilings in rooms. Their echoes add to the new sounds in the rooms. Ceilings made of tiles with little holes in them take in sound waves much as sponges soak up water. This cuts room noise down quite a bit. Carpets, curtains, and furniture also soak up sound waves. It's a fact that an empty room is full of echoes. A room with furniture is much quieter.

Putting machines on rubber pads can cut down noise by keeping tables and floors from shaking along with the machines. Their shaking adds to the noise from the machines.

Noise can also be blocked or stopped completely. That might seem like the best way to stop noise, but it is not always so. For example, to soundproof rooms means that walls and ceilings must be very thick and covered with soundproofing material. The extra building materials would make homes and apartments more expensive.

Cheaper and easier ways to cut down on unwanted noise need to be developed.

Recalling Facts

1. Loud noises can cause
   - ☐ a. dizziness.
   - ☐ b. ear pain.
   - ☐ c. sore throats.

2. Loud sounds that reach the inner ear may rip and tear
   - ☐ a. bone.
   - ☐ b. muscle.
   - ☐ c. tissue.

3. In order to stop noise, cars use
   - ☐ a. gas.
   - ☐ b. mufflers.
   - ☐ c. radiators.

4. Ceilings made of tiles with little holes in them take in
   - ☐ a. finger waves.
   - ☐ b. light waves.
   - ☐ c. sound waves.

5. In order to soundproof a room, the walls and ceilings must be very
   - ☐ a. clean.
   - ☐ b. smooth.
   - ☐ c. thick.

Understanding the Passage

6. This article is mostly about
   - ☐ a. car mufflers.
   - ☐ b. rubber pads.
   - ☐ c. unwanted noise.

7. Loud noises can cause
   - ☐ a. blindness.
   - ☐ b. hearing loss.
   - ☐ c. terrible headaches.

8. The weaker the sound wave, the
   - ☐ a. more harmful the sound.
   - ☐ b. louder the sound.
   - ☐ c. softer the sound.

9. When sound waves bounce off an object, they make
   - ☐ a. an echo.
   - ☐ b. a hole.
   - ☐ c. a ripple.

10. Soundproofing a room is
    - ☐ a. cheap.
    - ☐ b. easy.
    - ☐ c. expensive.

Happy, Healthy Teeth

Take care of your teeth and your teeth will take care of you. Your teeth are a living part of your body. They have nerves and blood vessels. Diseased teeth can cause pain, die, and fall out. False teeth often do not work as well as natural teeth. By knowing what causes dental diseases, you can learn to take proper care of your teeth. If you do take proper care of your teeth, you can keep them your entire life.

Plaque is the main enemy of healthy teeth. Everyone has plaque. It is a sticky, colorless film that coats the teeth. Plaque is always forming on the teeth, especially at the gumline. If plaque is not removed, it builds up and gets under the gumline. Plaque that is left on the teeth for some time hardens. The result is tooth decay and gum disease.

The bacteria in plaque live on sugar. They change sugar into acids which break down the tooth's hard enamel. If left untreated, decay goes deeper and deeper into the tooth. After a while, the decay reaches the nerves and blood vessels of the inner tooth. By the time this happens, the tooth has probably started to ache.

In addition to tooth decay, there are also gum diseases to watch out for. The bacteria in plaque make poisons that attack the gums. Small pockets form around the teeth. The pockets trap more bacteria and food particles. Finally, the bone supporting the teeth is attacked and starts to shrink. Teeth become loose and may fall out. Adults lose most teeth this way.

Gum disease starts slowly. There may be no pain. As a rule, gum disease first appears as a swelling. Then the gums become tender. There also may be bleeding. To heal diseased gums, your teeth need one or more dental cleanings. The cleanings must be following by good, regular care. Sometimes, gum disease starts with signs that are not so easy to see. Only a dentist can spot these signs. Regular visits to your dentist are a must.

Many people worry about bad breath. This may result from several causes. It could be due to gum disease or leftover bits of food lodged in the mouth. It may be caused by plaque coating the teeth, gums, and tongue. Decayed teeth can cause bad breath.

Keep your mouth healthy! When you brush your teeth, do a good job.

Recalling Facts

1. Teeth contain nerves and
   - ☐ a. blood vessels.
   - ☐ b. muscles.
   - ☐ c. skin tissue.

2. Plaque is always forming on the teeth, especially at the
   - ☐ a. crown.
   - ☐ b. gumline.
   - ☐ c. tip.

3. The bacteria in plaque live on
   - ☐ a. fat.
   - ☐ b. protein.
   - ☐ c. sugar.

4. Bacteria in plaque attack both teeth and
   - ☐ a. gums.
   - ☐ b. throat.
   - ☐ c. tongue.

5. Bad breath can be caused by
   - ☐ a. gum disease.
   - ☐ b. overeating.
   - ☐ c. sore throats.

Understanding the Passage

6. Choose the best title for this article.
   - ☐ a. Dentists Know Best
   - ☐ b. Tooth Decay and Gum Disease
   - ☐ c. Tongue and Cheek Diseases

7. This article hints that healthy teeth
   - ☐ a. have stronger enamel.
   - ☐ b. can last a lifetime.
   - ☐ c. often fall out.

8. Most tooth decay is caused by
   - ☐ a. bad breath.
   - ☐ b. plaque.
   - ☐ c. saliva.

9. Many adults lose their teeth because of
   - ☐ a. gum disease.
   - ☐ b. regular cleanings.
   - ☐ c. tooth decay.

10. We can see from this article that it is a good idea to
    - ☐ a. clean your teeth once a week.
    - ☐ b. use a popular mouthwash.
    - ☐ c. visit a dentist regularly.

It's never too late to start a weight-loss program. The guiding principle should be common sense. The diet should have a wide variety of ordinary foods. It can also include an occasional treat, such as cookies or cake. In this way, you can stick with the diet. Ideally, a person should try to loose only one or two pounds a week. Someone who loses more than that is losing excess fluid, not fat.

One of the worst ways to diet is to skip meals. Passing up breakfast makes you that much hungrier at lunchtime. Skipping meals also makes you want to snack. It can also enable you to make excuses for eating more at the next meal. At least three meals each day is preferred. Some people eat six small meals. This is fine if you don't increase your total intake of calories.

You should also eat slowly. There is a twenty minute lag between the time food is eaten and the time your brain responds. If you eat too fast, you may eat too much food before your brain registers a "satisfied" signal.

Exercise is an important part of a good weight-control program. During exercise you burn calories. For every 3,500 calories you burn, you lose a pound. But exercise provides a weight-control bonus. It seems that the body continues to burn calories at an increased rate after you stop exercising.

Exercise can also offset the body's response to less food. Some studies show that when you eat less, your metabolism slows.

Metabolism is the process by which your body turns food into energy. If you exercise while dieting, you can stop that effect. Exercising also helps you lose the right kind of weight. People who exercise while dieting lose more body fat. But people who diet without exercise lose muscle tissue as well.

The best exercises for beginners or inactive people include stretching and swimming. Another good exercise is walking. It can be done by nearly everyone in nearly every type of weather. The best rule of thumb is if you are too tired to talk while exercising, you are working too hard.

Proper weight control provides benefits like a slim body and more energy. An old saying is "An apple a day keeps the doctor away." But a good diet and exercise program are more likely to do the job.

Recalling Facts

1. The basic rule when beginning a weight-loss program is to
   - ☐ a. eat when you're hungry.
   - ☐ b. use common sense.
   - ☐ c. skip meals.

2. How many meals each day should you eat?
   - ☐ a. eight
   - ☐ b. three
   - ☐ c. one

3. What is the time lag between eating food and the brain's response?
   - ☐ a. 20 minutes
   - ☐ b. one hour
   - ☐ c. 5 minutes

4. When exercising, you burn
   - ☐ a. fluid.
   - ☐ b. calories.
   - ☐ c. food.

5. Proper exercise aids in losing
   - ☐ a. muscle tissue.
   - ☐ b. hair.
   - ☐ c. body fat.

Understanding the Passage

6. From this selection, we can say that
   - ☐ a. successful weight control gives you a trim body.
   - ☐ b. excess body fat is healthful.
   - ☐ c. excess body fluid is healthful.

7. Proper exercise makes dieting
   - ☐ a. more difficult.
   - ☐ b. easier.
   - ☐ c. more interesting.

8. This selection hints that
   - ☐ a. your body needs desserts every day.
   - ☐ b. fast weight loss is beneficial.
   - ☐ c. exercise and a proper diet are good for everyone.

9. The well-known saying "An apple a day keeps the doctor away" really means that
   - ☐ a. eating fruits will help keep you healthy.
   - ☐ b. eating apples is necessary for weight loss.
   - ☐ c. a diet of fruit is better than a good diet and exercise program.

10. The process of metabolism is how
    - ☐ a. you lose weight.
    - ☐ b. your body turns food into energy.
    - ☐ c. you can increase your intake of calories.

Answer Key

Progress Graph

Pacing Graph

Answer Key

	1.	2.	3.	4.	5.	6.	7.	8.	9.	10.
1	b	a	c	a	b	a	b	b	b	c
2	b	a	a	a	b	b	c	b	b	b
3	b	a	c	b	a	b	b	c	c	a
4	a	a	b	a	b	c	a	a	a	b
5	c	a	b	b	b	a	b	a	c	a
6	c	a	a	a	b	c	b	a	c	b
7	a	c	b	c	a	c	b	b	a	a
8	b	c	a	c	b	c	b	a	b	a
9	a	c	a	c	b	c	b	b	a	b
10	c	c	c	c	a	c	b	c	b	b
11	b	a	a	c	b	c	a	c	a	b
12	b	b	a	c	c	a	b	b	c	a
13	a	c	b	a	b	c	a	b	c	c
14	c	a	b	c	a	a	b	a	b	c
15	c	c	a	b	c	b	c	b	b	b
16	a	c	b	a	b	a	c	a	a	b
17	b	a	b	a	a	c	b	b	b	c
18	c	c	a	c	a	c	c	a	c	b
19	a	b	c	c	a	c	c	a	c	b
20	c	a	a	a	b	c	b	b	b	a
21	c	b	b	b	a	b	b	c	a	c
22	b	b	c	c	c	a	a	b	b	c
23	a	b	c	a	a	c	b	a	c	a
24	b	a	c	b	b	b	b	a	b	b
25	c	b	c	c	c	a	b	b	c	c

26	1. a	2. b	3. b	4. b	5. a	6. a	7. a	8. b	9. c	10. c
27	1. c	2. a	3. a	4. a	5. b	6. a	7. a	8. a	9. b	10. c
28	1. c	2. a	3. c	4. b	5. c	6. a	7. b	8. b	9. c	10. a
29	1. c	2. c	3. a	4. c	5. b	6. c	7. c	8. a	9. a	10. b
30	1. a	2. b	3. a	4. c	5. c	6. c	7. b	8. b	9. b	10. c
31	1. b	2. b	3. b	4. a	5. c	6. b	7. a	8. a	9. a	10. c
32	1. c	2. c	3. a	4. b	5. b	6. b	7. a	8. c	9. b	10. a
33	1. c	2. b	3. b	4. b	5. c	6. b	7. b	8. a	9. c	10. a
34	1. a	2. a	3. b	4. c	5. b	6. a	7. a	8. a	9. c	10. b
35	1. b	2. c	3. b	4. b	5. a	6. a	7. a	8. b	9. a	10. c
36	1. c	2. a	3. c	4. c	5. b	6. a	7. a	8. b	9. a	10. a
37	1. c	2. a	3. b	4. b	5. c	6. b	7. c	8. b	9. b	10. a
38	1. a	2. a	3. c	4. a	5. a	6. b	7. b	8. a	9. c	10. a
39	1. a	2. b	3. c	4. a	5. a	6. a	7. b	8. a	9. c	10. c
40	1. b	2. b	3. a	4. b	5. a	6. b	7. a	8. b	9. c	10. c
41	1. a	2. c	3. b	4. a	5. b	6. c	7. c	8. b	9. b	10. c
42	1. a	2. b	3. a	4. b	5. c	6. a	7. a	8. a	9. c	10. c
43	1. c	2. b	3. c	4. c	5. c	6. c	7. b	8. a	9. a	10. c
44	1. c	2. b	3. b	4. a	5. c	6. a	7. b	8. c	9. c	10. a
45	1. b	2. c	3. b	4. b	5. a	6. c	7. a	8. a	9. a	10. b
46	1. b	2. b	3. c	4. b	5. b	6. b	7. b	8. a	9. b	10. b
47	1. b	2. c	3. c	4. c	5. a	6. b	7. c	8. c	9. b	10. c
48	1. b	2. c	3. b	4. c	5. c	6. c	7. b	8. c	9. a	10. c
49	1. a	2. b	3. c	4. a	5. a	6. b	7. b	8. b	9. a	10. c
50	1. b	2. b	3. a	4. b	5. c	6. a	7. b	8. c	9. a	10. b

Progress Graph (1–25)

Directions: Write your comprehension score in the box under the selection number. Then put an x on the line above each box to show your reading time and words-per-minute reading rate.

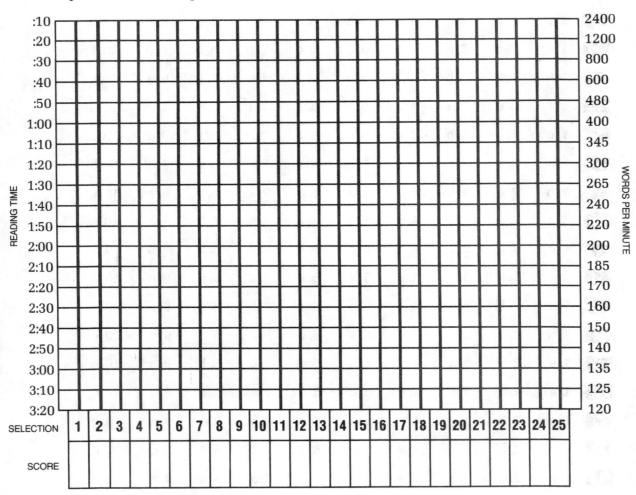

Progress Graph (26–50)

Directions: Write your comprehension score in the box under the selection number. Then put an x on the line above each box to show your reading time and words-per-minute reading rate.

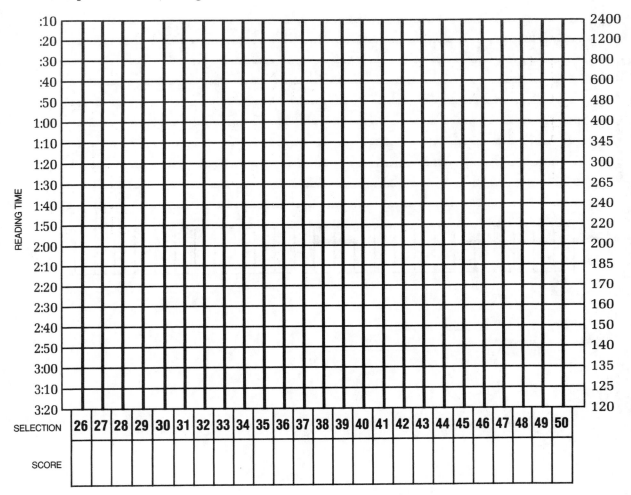

Pacing Graph

Directions: In the boxes labeled "Pace" along the bottom of the graph, write your words-per-minute rate. On the vertical line above each box, put an x to indicate your comprehension score.

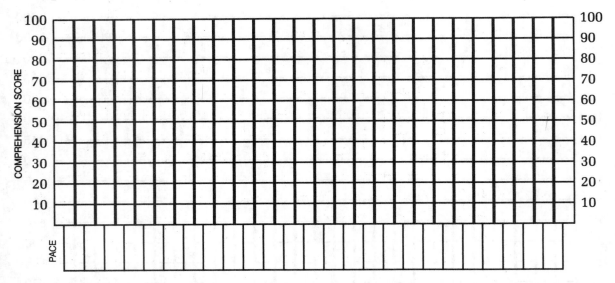